MEDIA STUDIES

THE BASICS

'This a great book ... it provides a clear and comprehensive account of the subject ... is very up to date and the reader will come away from it with a good understanding of key issues in Media Studies.'

Marcus Leaning, University of Winchester, UK

There have been seismic shifts in what constitutes the media in recent years with technological advances ushering in whole new categories of producers, consumers and modes of delivery. This has been reflected in the way media is studied with new theories, concepts and practices coming to the fore. *Media Studies: The Basics* is the ideal guide to this changing landscape and addresses core questions including:

* Who, or what, are the media?
* What are the key terms and concepts used in analysing media?
* Where have been the impacts of the globalization of media?
* How, and by whom, is media made in the 21st century?

Featuring contemporary case studies from around the world, a glossary and suggestions for further reading, this is the ideal introduction to media studies today.

Dr Julian McDougall is Reader in Education in the Centre for Developmental and Applied Research in Education at the University of Wolverhampton. He is editor of the *Media Education Research Journal*, author of a range of course textbooks, *The Media Teacher's Book*, *Studying Videogames* and *After the Media: Culture and Identity in the 21st Century* (Routledge).

The Basics

MEDIA STUDIES

THE BASICS

Julian McDougall

Routledge
Taylor & Francis Group

LONDON AND NEW YORK

First published 2012
by Routledge
2 Park Square, Milton Park, Abingdon, Oxon OX14 4RN

Simultaneously published in the USA and Canada
by Routledge
711 Third Avenue, New York, NY 10017

Routledge is an imprint of the Taylor & Francis Group, an informa business

British Library Cataloguing in Publication Data
A catalogue record for this book is available from the British Library

Library of Congress Cataloging in Publication Data
McDougall, Julian.
    Media studies : the basics / Julian McDougall.
        p. cm. – (The basics)
    Includes bibliographical references and index.
    1. Mass media. I. Title.
    P91.25.M3645 2012
    302.23–dc23
                            2011045288

ISBN: 978-0-415-68126-1 (hbk)
ISBN: 978-0-415-68125-4 (pbk)
ISBN: 978-0-203-11954-9 (ebk)

Typeset in Bembo and Scala Sans
by Taylor & Francis Books

Printed and bound in Great Britain by
TJ International Ltd, Padstow, Cornwall

CONTENTS

LIST OF FIGURES

ACKNOWLEDGEMENTS

To Alex, for caring and unsung wisdom and humility.

To Lyd and Ned for the point of it all. To Stanley for the uncomplicated understanding.

In 1992, I funded a Masters degree by working in a campus bookshop in a 'Northern industrial town'. The biggest selling book during my time there was *Philosophy: The Basics* by Nigel Warburton, which I read during breaks.

In 2011, Routledge sent me Warburton's latest edition to help fit my ideas for this book into this series.

The journey from selling 'Basics' titles to writing one was made in a bygone era, I fear. After comprehensive school, I went on to FE and took a National Diploma in Media which led to Polytechnic (with no tuition fees and a grant to support my living costs) and then eventually to Ph.D., a job in higher education, a research post and a range of publications, including this.

So – in recognition of all those who participated in the expansion of education before the ladder was pulled back up.

Respect is also due, as they say, to Media Studies comrades I've worked with and learned from over the years – Pete Fraser, Wayne O'Brien, Clive Edwards, Steve Dixon, Richard Sanders, Richard Berger, Mark Readman, Pete Bennett and Julie Courage-Dixon.

INTRODUCTION

Maybe you have picked up this book because you're starting a course in Media Studies (given the title, it's a fair guess). Perhaps you are an English teacher and you are going to 'pick up' some media teaching and need to be one step ahead of the students. Or you could be a parent, wondering what Media Studies is really all about and whether your child should spend their time engaging with it. Or you could be such a polymath that you have no vocational reason or vested interest whatsoever. It would be nice to think that some of you are in that last category.

If you are a media student, the assumption will be that you've never studied it before (although it might be a useful 'refresher' even if you have). All the way through, the emphasis will be on distinguishing between everyday media engagement and critical media literacy. Just by being alive in the contemporary 'mediated' world, we all respond actively to media – we never just 'take it in' without any thought or interpretation. Equally, the distinction between our 'real world' experiences and media experiences are not always clear-cut. Media are, for most people, part of our 'lifeworld'. We refer to media in our conversations, use media as reference points in all kinds of ways and increasingly respond to, adapt or even create media for public reception through YouTube and other 'Web 2.0' affordances. But the critical media student brings to this everyday engagement a range of academic theories and approaches. Textual analysis is the practice of deconstructing media products to understand how they are constructed and how people receive them in different ways. Theories of media and power look at ownership, control, regulation and politics in historical and economic contexts. Put simply, who controls media and does controlling media equate to controlling us? In a democracy, what should media be *for*? Academic approaches to media globalization go beyond 'the global village' to explore the role media play in blending local, national and international identities. Theories of change are all about technology – the idea of 'Media 2.0' and claims and counterclaims about the impact on new social media on how we communicate, engage with the public world and, ultimately, how we think. There are plentiful 'brave new world' theories and plentiful counterarguments – words of caution. There are optimistic and dystopian theories about the future and the next generation of media students will doubtless look back at all this with amusement. But, as they say, we are where we are. If all these theoretical areas aren't enough to deal with, media students need to create their own media as well and present this in a 'theorizing' context, reflecting on the creative process and taking a step back from their own products to do textual analysis on them.

Hopefully, we are done with the 'soft option' idea already.

A BRIEF HISTORY

I like to think of the history of Media Studies through hip hop song titles.

In the first phase of the subject – from the 1960s to the 1980s – it was generally accepted that the media had lots of power over people and this was probably quite often a bad thing, so Media Studies would help people 'resist' this power. At this time, Media Studies was dominated by the study of 'mass media' – 'Television, the drug of the nation'. I studied media during this phase. Practical work was a part of it, but it needed, as Gauntlett describes it 'Big Stuff', which meant lots of time in edit suites doing 'crash editing'. Exciting, but very hard to produce impressive work.

In the second phase (1990s and the first part of the 21st century, pre-broadband), Media Studies passed beyond 'the relevance boom' into an era of digital creativity, making use of affordable and accessible technology to give students the chance to develop production skills in order to imitate conventions of 'real' media products and/or to gain entry into 'the media' for employment.

Phase three – the online age, where we are now, contains features of the previous two stages but with one fundamental shift – the Internet. This allows us to see much more clearly the dynamic relationship between media producers, audiences, critical fans and amateur 'prosumers'. Nobody is saying that the Internet has changed everything for everyone (here's a sobering thought – most people in the world don't have it), but it has made the distinction between 'the media' and 'us' harder to hold on to. So we are, if you like, now doing Media Studies 'after the media'. This is where you come in.

HOW THE BOOK WORKS

Most Media courses are organized into discrete elements, ranging from 'Television Studies' to 'Game Design' and more abstract areas like 'Postmodernism'. You will notice that the chapters of this book are arranged on broader thematic lines. This is so you can apply these 'macro' ideas to the detail, whatever that might be – and Media Studies is a huge 'horizontal discourse', so any other approach would skew this introduction too much towards one way of doing it.

Each chapter starts with a set of key objectives for your under-standing and then takes you through a set of academic approaches, contemporary examples and more detailed case studies. This provides a template, for you to adapt to your own areas of interest. It's an introduction, of course, to 'the basics' – so as you develop as a critical student of media, you will take these 'entry level' explorations and make them your own, take them in your own new directions and go beyond them. That said, each chapter is written with an eye on the framing 'benchmarks' for all undergraduate media courses, so they will serve as a reliable toolkit for studying media in any context at this level.

A couple of years ago, I was invited onto the BBC's *Today Programme* to talk about the subject and immediately commanded to 'defend your discipline'. I replied, to the amusement of the presenter that I was bored with being asked to do so. But it's true. I've been teaching, researching and writing about media now for 20 years. It dominates my life and any distinction between engaging with media 'for pleasure' and doing it for work have been eroded beyond reconstruction (a very postmodern existence). It's easy enough to watch *The X Factor* with my family and, at the same time, think about 'interpellation'. I can do that because I had some great media teachers when I was much younger. But, still, never a week goes by when I don't get asked what Media Studies is and/or why people should do it.

I hope that reading this book will provide you with the answers to those 'boring' questions and to help you get started. Much more exciting is this – you are now a part of Media Studies, a catalyst, an agent in its future. Use the power for good.

Julian McDougall
June 2011.

1

STUDYING MEDIA
WHY, WHAT, HOW AND WHO?

AIMS

This chapter will introduce you to:

* a range of different approaches to studying media;
* the history of media and of Media Studies;
* the most important theoretical concepts used by students of media.

MEDIATION

Welcome to the study of everyday life – yours, mine, and everybody else's. If you are looking at this book expecting to find out about 'the media' – and not about the mundane stuff of ordinary human existence, then this opening statement will have surprised you, perhaps, and you might be confused. But welcome anyway.

The point is that media are so central to our existence that we can't really separate 'the media' from everything else and bracket off the moments when we are engaging with media and the rest of our waking hours.

* Do we see 'going online' as something we have to make time for?
* Do we notice every advertisement and acknowledge its methods of persuasion and the degree to which it succeeds?

* Are we able to distinguish between 'physical' experiences of reality and the ideas we get from media?
* Can we separate screen reading from traditional text reading?
* Are our Facebook friends just virtual?

Most of the time, those of us that have access to fast-speed Internet and mobile devices live in a kind of 'blended reality' and all sorts of media dominate the lives we lead – our lives, then are 'mediated', we live in a 'media environment':

> Media Studies starts from the observation that media now permeate almost every moment of our existence. There is almost nothing that we do that escapes mediation.

> (Press and Williams 2010: 194)

To some extent, this has been the case for a long time, ever since mass communication allowed people to relate their own lives to everyone else's through shared media on a broad scale – in the form of newspapers and printed texts in the first place (reaching large audiences, as opposed to cave drawings and other earlier representations of human experience, which couldn't be shared across space and time). But it's clear that this 'mediation' is becoming more and more endemic as technology affords (for better or worse) a more mobile and constant, 24/7 engagement with media. De Zengotita offers a really far-reaching version of this 'mediation' idea, suggesting that we have been transported to 'a place where everything is addressed to us, everything is for us, and nothing is beyond us anymore' (De Zengotita 2005: 11).

This idea, which we will come back to later when we explore '**postmodernism**', describes a time period that we are apparently in, when there is no longer any distinction between reality, ourselves and media – this is the extreme end of 'mediation' and one important challenge for the media student is to develop an informed perspective on this – not only 'is it true', but if it is, is it the case everywhere, for everyone or in some places, for some people but not others? Is it **global** or does it depend on culture, geography, economics and politics?

So rather than kick off with a simple history of the media, we need to look at the history of *ideas* about media and their importance in society. So this chapter will present a chronological account of how our idea of 'the media' has developed from the printing press to augmented reality and, alongside this history, how Media Studies has emerged, developed and expanded as an academic response to the importance of media in society. In addition, the question *of* Media Studies itself and its status in contemporary education – hugely popular but sometimes controversial – will be explored. The chapter will move on to offer an overview of who or what constitute *contemporary* media – the field of study for the coming years – and an introduction to the key conceptual toolkit needed for such analysis, which will then be covered in detail throughout the rest of the book.

WHY *STUDY* MEDIA?

> Media Studies has 'failed' to change the world in some respects but it has had one significant victory – it is now possible to study popular culture like *This is England* within the formal education system.
>
> (Stafford 2010: 10)

This statement says a lot about Media Studies and how it is different to other academic subjects. We can draw out three key ideas that are important to understand about the discipline.

Firstly, the idea that studying something called **'popular' culture** in schools, colleges and universities is a recent possibility. This suggests that education changes to respond to changing times, which is on one level obvious (what counts as 'history' for example, must be constantly updated, and literature studies will accommodate recent works of fiction into 'the canon'). But it does mean that Media Studies can be understood as a reaction to the growth of 'the media' and there are all sorts of implications to that, as we shall see.

Second, the claim that that this is a 'victory' that must, then, have been fought for. Why would that be a big deal? What is 'popular' culture and why has it been traditional to study 'high culture' (litera-ture, classical music, theatre, fine art) but only to 'consume' popular (or 'mass') culture such as films. Popular culture is different to high culture in the sense that it doesn't have a 'canon' – a set of 'great works' that students must learn to 'appreciate' – and so this makes it more difficult for the general public to understand subjects that put popular culture into the curriculum. It is, after all, generally accepted, that Shakespeare is somehow 'good for you', whether you like it or not (a bit like fish and broccoli, many children would say). Popular culture, on the other hand, has the image of being 'just entertainment' and we understand education and entertainment as being necessarily disconnected. Lacey (2011) suggests that there is much in common between Dickens and soap opera so, democratically, they might be given equal weight in/by education, and goes on (2011: 46) to suggest that the proliferation of 'greatest ever' lists circulated between consumers of popular culture eventually have the same kind of effect as their more highbrow canonical counterparts. No matter what the medium, genre or subgenre, we end up being told what we should consider to be the most valuable products within it.

How might this be political in the sense that we might start to question the way that education is organized into subjects and 'legitimate' areas of study? When commanded on Radio 4's *Today Programme* to 'defend your discipline', we get the idea that what we are doing is controversial in some ways, or at least that some people are confused about the purpose of bringing 'everyday culture' into classrooms and lecture theatres.

Third, the idea that Media Studies might want to 'change the world'. Would we expect mathematics teachers to talk in this way? Perhaps, in the sense that making people more numerate would be a good thing, but probably not in the same way that Stafford means – there is a notion, then, that Media Studies – in its creating of more 'media literate' citizens, is somehow a bigger project. Maybe this just gives Media teachers (me included) a greater sense of self-importance which, given the Radio 4 example above, we probably need! Or perhaps, if we accept that 'the media' does influence us and go some way towards constructing our ideologies of the world and the people around us, then studying media critically ought to be considered a serious and important project for any mature democracy. Discuss!

STARTING POINTS

So, assuming that you are reading this book because you intend to study media, you have probably a fairly clear idea of why that would be a good use of your time (and money, most likely). Taking Stafford's ideas further, we will find that rationales for Media

Studies tend to be framed by three discourses (way of making sense of things in language that come to construct accepted 'common sense' ideas about the world). These discourses sometimes combine and sometimes they conflict with one another.

THE 'POWERFUL MEDIA' DISCOURSE

This is to do with the influence and effects that media have in our contemporary lives. If something is influential and powerful, then knowing how it works and how it operates is important. Within this discourse, Media Studies can take its place among similar areas of knowledge such as politics, environmental studies, history (if you accept that the past has influence on the present) and even astrophysics.

THE ECONOMIC DISCOURSE

There are jobs for creative and technically gifted people in media sectors and there are jobs for media-savvy people in all areas of the economy, so within this way of thinking, Media Studies exists to equip its students with **creative skills** that can help them in the jobs market on graduating.

THE 'MEDIA LITERACY' DISCOURSE

Understood within this discourse, media students are better equipped to communicate in the modern world if they have the analytical skills to critically interpret media texts – this makes Media Studies a kind of extension of English, but it also combines with the 'Powerful Media' discourse when it carries a **protectionist** weight – that is, when it is argued that people are better able to resist the power of 'the media' if they are media literate. Equally, we can put the 'Powerful Media' together with the economic discourse — one of the reasons why media is powerful is because it is big business and because politicians are arguably as concerned with media 'spin' as they are with policies. And we can connect 'media literacy' to economics when we understand literacy as active and creative – communicating effectively in new media environments is increasingly important for employers.

On the other hand, though, there are tensions between these ways of understanding the subject – some courses are far more critical and academic, while others are more skills-based and creative. And if students can choose options within those courses, then it is difficult to say which version of Media Studies is at work. The most common rift is between the economic discourse and the others – if students are to be critical of media influence, then this doesn't sit comfortably with the idea that they should be 'trained up' to be part of the process they are critiquing.

You may question why we are putting 'the media' in these inverted commas here. The reason is that the idea of 'the media' is quite complex and needs some unpacking before we can go ahead with an introduction to Media Studies. So what follows is not simply a history of 'the media' but rather a history of how people have understood it, what people have thought it to be, over time. It's a chronological account of how media have changed – and how this has impacted on the study of media – over time, from the printing press to mass literacy to the advent of television, the emergence of videogames and finally to broadband internet – and the hotly contested argument that at this point the audience begin to make media for themselves. Many readers of this book will be undertaking, or preparing to start out on, undergraduate Media Studies courses. Berger and McDougall (2010) write about Media Studies in higher education and in particular the obsession many university departments have had with sticking to 'single media' courses, ignoring the ways in which broader patterns of production, distribution and consumption might render such a view as outdated. Perhaps this is something you can apply to your own degree course?

So, you will have got the idea by now that Media Studies is the outcome of a range of responses to the development of media in society and that there is a degree of ongoing dialogue about how it should work and what students should *do*. This isn't a bad thing – academic enquiry is all about discussion and argument. And as we will see next, the debate goes on.

WHAT *ARE* MEDIA?

Media Studies is concerned with the relationship between people, media, life and society and looks at these relationships in a number of ways. There are quantitative and environmental questions about who is making use of what media and then qualitative questions about how they interpret media and its function in their lives. *Change* is a constant factor in this kind of enquiry. Then there is the question of **access**, **power** and **democracy** – who owns and controls media and what kinds of power might be exercised through such structural features as concentrated ownership and corporate agendas? The 2011 *News of the World* phone-hacking scandal in the UK brings this to light very clearly, so the power and influence of media has perhaps never been more prominent in public discussion. Media Studies is also concerned with the nature of media **texts** and a range of approaches to textual reception allow the media student to 'deconstruct' the ways in which meaning is made in and between texts. This is informed by studies of media audiences with particular regard to demographics such as local or national culture, gender, sexuality, age, social class and ability/disability. Sometimes these areas of focus are separated in Media Studies courses (for example, a unit on Textual Analysis, a module on Media Ownership or a coursework project on Female Film Reception) but often they are connected, and in that way a student of media needs *synoptic* skill – making connections, synthesis, dialogue between ideas.

PRINT

Although the history of people communicating with each other goes much further back and some histories of the media (defined as communication over a distance) begin in 776 BC with carrier pigeons, when we want to measure the importance of a new technology that changes or enhances the ways in which we can communicate, we tend to talk about the advent of the printing press as the one to measure new developments against. This was attributed to Gutenberg in 1455. Once the printed word could be mass-produced on a broad scale, 'mass literacy' was the outcome.

IMAGES

Photography didn't arrive – adding the tools with which people can capture real life and preserve events in this way – for another 350 years, which is staggering when you consider the pace of more recent change, as we will discuss. In 1843 (according to historical accounts), the primitive affordances of 'Morse Code' were developed into the more sophisticated telegraph – this was the first example of sending information (words) through space (using a wire) to arrive without much of a time-delay, something we take for granted, of course, 24/7, in our 'always-connected' lives.

COMMUNICATIONS

When the telephone was created in 1876, not only text on paper, but also real-time sounds (words, discussions, exchanged verbally) could be sent and received through a wire. Not long after, in 1898, photography was further developed into moving images in the form of film. This was probably the most amazing invention for people to come to terms with – it has become a well-worn cliché, which may have been embellished, but the historical narrative tells us that people were terrified when viewing a train approaching on a screen as they were unable to comprehend the distinction between reality and moving images. You will notice that, as we move forward, the time between technological changes decreases – it took more than 300 years to go from the printing press to photography, but only 80 years or so to develop still photographs into moving images. This 'change acceleration' continues strikingly as we move through history.

MOVING PICTURES

Film is invented in the late 19th century. So consider it this way – it is only around 125 years since film was invented, so that is very recent in the history of the human race, but the progress made from the Lumiere Brothers' film of the train approaching to *Avatar* in 3D is striking in such a space of time (but unimpressive in relation to the pace of progress in the broadband age).

Media Studies has traditionally been concerned with 'mass media'. As we will see, some argue that's an outdated concept in the era of Facebook and YouTube, but the subject was certainly designed to put the study of media texts, which were seen to have some influence over large groups of people into the curriculum. Mass media really began with the printing press, clearly, but because Media Studies and English have been kept apart, our subject has tended to see its origins as being in the early part of the 20th century, when both film and radio became mass media and their products were 'decoded' by large audiences all watching or listening at the same time and, as a result, celebrities were created and given the status of icons – people whose screen/sound characteristics resonated with the public and represented issues of the time in ways which Media academics could analyse as culturally significant. But Media Studies came out of more general theories of communication, originating in the US in the 1930s and then developed further (for obvious reasons) in response to the use made by the Nazis of 'propaganda' as a means of persuading a mass audience.

THE BLACK BOX

Television, now claimed by commentators to be 'in decline' and certainly in a period of online reinvention (in a 'post-broadcast' era, with some notable mass-rating exceptions) arrived in the middle of the last century, in black and white and with a small number of channels in most countries and periods of 'down time' when nothing was scheduled. Outside of the **public service broadcasting** sector (in the UK, the BBC, funded by the licence fee as a form of taxation in order to preserve independence and the values of entertainment, education and information in equal measure), the commercial potential of television – for the obvious reason that the TV set is in our homes – was harnessed and survived as a lucrative market until the era of 'on demand' and the possibility of fast-forwarding through the commercial break led, in recent years, to a move toward online advertising. It's worth pausing here to note that until the late 1990s, very few media commentators, analysts or academics saw any real connection between media (TV, film, radio, news) and computers, which were still categorized as tools for work or domestic administration – in most homes, computers were put into offices or spare rooms, with office furniture signifying their status, very different from the 'shrine' of the family television with its ever-growing screen size and comfortable surroundings.

EFFECTS

Media analysis (still not formally arranged as an academic subject) was largely focused on effects and behaviour in the 1940s and

1950s. As we shall see later in this book, the '**effects model**' is still prevalent in popular discourse, with a recent spate of interest in 'internet addiction' but among Media academics this way of looking at audience responses has been largely discredited, with notable attacks coming from Gauntlett (1998) and Barker and Petley (1998):

> Predictably, each new claim comes with an imprimatur of 'this time we've done it, this time we've finally proved it' – but never does an admission follow, when their claims fall apart (as they invariably do) that they were simply wrong in the first place.
>
> (Barker and Petley 1998: 2)

Cinema survived various threats from the 1950s to the present day – first, the TV would kill the big-screen experience, then the VCR definitely would, but by the time DVD and then Blu-Ray arrived, the social arena of the multiplex, surround sound, IMAX and 3D had all played their part in recharging audiences' desires to see films together on big screens. This is important for us because we should learn from history to be sceptical about the claims made for how each new technology or mode of media consumption will replace entirely what came before – the current version of this well-worn mantra relates to the future of newspapers and printed books, although you might think there is a much clearer distinction between watching a film on a laptop screen and in a 3D cinema than there is between reading a printed book and an electronic 'Kindle' version.

Media Studies arrived in the 1960s, as a formal academic subject with qualifications (or at least 'modes of delivery' within the curriculum) and at this time it took its theoretical template from a range of models of the 'active audience' such as cultivation theory and uses and gratifications but, at the same time, a view of the 'all powerful media' remained – with a focus on ideology, hegemony and, from McLuhan, the framing nature of media in our consciousness – 'the medium is the message'. Writing a long time before new digital media, McLuhan's idea was that the technology (television, for example) that brings us media content actively shapes our perceptions of reality:

McLuhan, concerned with the connecting impulse of media, is cited by many as being something of a 'prophet' – foreseeing the impact of the internet long before it arrived (see Levinson 2001). Although his work is retrospectively 'repackaged' to consider media power in both **protectionist** and **emancipatory** ways, it is clear that he was influential in developing an approach to media as form – rather than just its content – and that he was optimistic about technology:

> The introduction to the 30th anniversary edition of *Understanding Media* noted that much of what McLuhan had to say made a good deal more sense in 1994 than it did in 1964.
>
> (Scannell 2007: 139)

Others are critical of his '**technological determinism**' – the assumption that technology in itself can bring cultural change without changes to broader structures – this debate rages on with regard to such recent examples as Wikileaks and the use of social media during political struggle in hitherto highly censorious nations.

IDEOLOGY

For media commentators and academics looking at things from the perspective of ideology (broadly speaking a **Marxist** view), media students' work is to identify ways in which 'the media' are used by the powerful to 'manufacture consent' (Chomsky 2002). This works in two ways – by representing news events in particular ways that justify the actions of the powerful and marginalize the opposition to such actions from the powerless, and by distracting us from the really important power struggles in our lives with 'tranquillizing' tools such as television:

> ... the bewildered herd basically just have to be distracted. Turn their attention to something else. Keep them out of trouble. Make sure that they remain at most spectators of action.
>
> (Chomsky 2002: 19)

This has remained (rightly) an important aspect of Media Studies – as the subject was partly developed out of a scrutiny of the Nazi use of propaganda, current debates about media power tend to oscillate between the position that 'the media' has ceased to exist as a dominant agency of power, because of the complexity of the new 'convergence culture' (Jenkins 2006) and the view that the powerful simply find ways of using the new social media to reinforce the existing power structures – the term for this is '**hegemony**':

> A state of hegemony is achieved when a provisional alliance of certain social groups exerts a consensus that makes the power of the dominant group appear both natural and legitimate. Institutions such as the mass media, the family, the education system and religion, play a key role in the shaping of people's awareness and consciousness and thus can be agents through which hegemony is constructed, exercised and maintained.
> (Watson and Hill 2003: 126)

As we shall see in the chapter on Powerful Media, hegemony and its alternative – **plurality** – have come into great prominence in the last year in the wake of the challenges to Rupert Murdoch's media empire in response to the *News of the World* phone-hacking scandal.

Stanley Cohen's 1972 book *Folk Devils and Moral Panics* is the most cited example of a sociological approach to subcultures and behaviour that is partly a response to media representation. Cohen was writing about young people in the days of mods, rockers and punks and his focus was on a range of elements that made up 'semiotic resistance' to mainstream ideology – music, clothes, drugs, behaviour. In this classic model, he found that newspaper exaggeration of 'deviant' behaviour (a **moral panic**) would lead to the 'deviant' group in question playing up to and amplifying the deviance and a much broader group of young people joining in than was/would have been the case prior to the moral panic. More recently, there have been a host of media moral panics, perhaps ironically about certain forms of media. In the 1980s there were 'video nasties', arising from the distorted representation of the Jamie Bulger murder as being 'caused' by *Child's Play 3* (there remains no evidence that this film was viewed by the children who murdered Bulger). Videogame violence (and addiction) has been the subject of an ongoing moral panic for decades and more recently the dangers of the internet for children have been the cause of a widespread but poorly articulated discourse of 'concern'. Sue Palmer's *Toxic*

Childhood remains, at the time of writing, the clearest example of this particular panic and in 2008, Tanya Byron was commissioned by the Labour Government of the time to produce a comprehensive review of the dangers of new media and, in particular, videogames for children. The Byron Review (2008) came to the following conclusions:

> It is vitally important that the sole or primary cause of violence or other behaviours such as excessive use in children is not identified as the media or video games per se. Neither should the media be seen as playing no role. Many researchers are now arguing for a more comprehensive approach to these questions of social importance, which begin with an account of the problem or behaviour of interest (e.g. aggression) and carry out a comprehensive examination of all the factors that might impact on that, including the influence of the media.
>
> (Byron 2008: 158)

One strand of Media Studies, then, has been – and always will be – concerned with the relationship between either 'the media' (in the case of the broader **ideological** approaches, informed by Chomsky and others) or various forms of media and 'the audience' or individuals in a society making use of media. And an aspect of this is the analysis of various kinds of 'effects'. These are broad, 'macro' questions for Media students to explore.

CULTURAL STUDIES

From the beginnings of media research and analysis in the 1930s, through to the development of Media Studies as a popular academic subject in the 1980s and 1990s, this interest in the influence of media at a 'macro' level was generally combined with textual analysis and the subsequent practical construction of texts at the micro. The work of the Centre for Contemporary Cultural Studies in Birmingham, England was formative (see Hall 1980) because it provided specific case studies of how audience decoding of media texts' encodings was related to structural factors – age, gender, social class, occupation. Morley's seminal *Nationwide* study (1981) showed how different groups responded in different ways to the 'preferred reading' of this mainstream, current affairs/news programme and that these responses seemed to be influenced by their demographic and professional profiles. The sustained influence of Morley's work, along with Hall's, is demonstrated by a recent 'remix' of this study, which was attempted (McDougall 2010) by applying the *Nationwide* model to American drama *The Wire*.

STRUCTURALISM

In the 1960s and 1970s, the structuralist 'semiotic' approach became hugely influential and has remained so at the micro, textual level. Barthes' 'classic' *Mythologies* (1984) was not explicitly focused on media but it contributed a way of looking at language, images, signs and symbols that helped media analysts to consider the ways in which our responses to media texts are framed by our reading of a symbolic language that is entirely cultural and based on oppositions and relations between significations. In other words, it is the difference between things, not the properties of individual things, that constructs meaning – you need to understand the whole system (which Barthes calls 'myth') to decode a single sign:

> Signs, far from 'naturally' or simply 'labelling' the real world, are socially constructed, and never as 'natural' as they seem. Semiotic approaches rightly suggest there is no neat boundary between the real and the imagined, indeed that they interpenetrate one another.
>
> (Branston and Stafford 2010: 23)

Understood in this way, everything we see is a sign, and it 'carries' a meaning. The basic meaning of the sign that most people can recognize and agree on, is known as the signifier. The more complex individual meanings that people give to signs are known as the signified. At a simple level, this approach was influential in forming the concept of 'media language', which refers to written, verbal, non-verbal, aural and aesthetic communication and usually a combination of these. For example, in television drama, a phone conversation between two characters in different locations can only be understood by the audience because of the relationship between the camera angles (close-ups, head and shoulder shots or longer shots showing location context), non-verbal performance (facial expressions during the phone conversation) and dialogue (what they say), lighting (to provide a meaningful atmosphere), editing (so we can follow the conversation and so that continuity is correct) and sound (atmospheric music or 'diegetic' sound such as a door opening). When we watch television, we don't need to think about these things, so they are unobtrusive. What we see appears to be straightforward and conventional. Over time, we come to expect certain styles of filming, acting, editing and sound for certain types of programme. So we can 'read' the **media language** as easily as we can understand our friends in conversations without having to recall the meaning of every word.

Post-structuralism departed from structuralism with an emphasis on trying to resist generalizing systems in order to spend more time looking for differences – for example, Butler's *Gender Trouble* (1990) asserts that gender is entirely cultural and that we perform gender differences in our daily lives. In Media Studies, at the micro level, students look at films, TV programmes, websites, videogames and 'deconstruct' the ways in which these texts make sense by combining signifiers that we think we recognize as related to the real world but are, at least partly, '**mythological**'.

Many of the key concepts that provide a framework for Media Studies – genre, narrative, representation and ideology are informed by a structuralist approach – the relationship between genre conventions, narrative themes, 'stock' representations and how these cultivate dominant ideas about people and places. But it is difficult for Media Studies to remain at the **micro** or even textual level for very long because, unlike many other subjects, it is already connected to *everything* that media represent, and as such it can never be completely self-regarding. Media are often cited as being a major force in the development of globalization so in this sense they are connected to politics, economics and geography. Consider this statement from the famous media analyst, campaigner and journalist John Pilger and you can see how difficult it would be to decouple analysis of media from analysis of much broader **macro** structures in the modern world:

> One of the most pervasive myths is that we live in an 'information age'. We actually live in a media age, in which most of the available information is repetitive, politically safe and is limited by invisible boundaries. Certainly, media technology, such as the 'digital revolution', may appear

to offer more choice and greater horizons, yet the media itself is actually shrinking in terms both of its ownership and editorial agenda or worldview.

(Pilger 2001: 15)

GLOBAL MEDIA

For a contemporary 'case study', to study the media reporting of political unrest in Libya in 2011, we would need to know something about politics in Libya. And this means that there is a need to try to retain an 'international' perspective on media. To trace the development of global media, in the 1980s, theories of **globalization** became important as technological change (satellite television) combined with political changes in Africa, Asia and South America to create new 'hybrid media products' (McMillin 2007) that combined successful formats from Western television series with local elements to 'translate' more successfully (as 'glocalized' versions) into these new territories. The impact of such cultural importing has been viewed as more or less positive depending on which theory of globalisation or **'cultural imperialism'** frames the analysis but one constant problem has been the way that looking at 'Third World' media developments from a Western vantage point often reduces the developing nation to the status of 'the other' and so the voices of the people are marginalized as they are spoken 'on behalf of' by researchers. More sustained **ethnographic** research, whereby media academics spend longer in the 'situated' context of media consumption has been seen as a solution to this problem, described by McMillin as:

> ... the importance of putting the media in their place in the social lives of their consumers. The intersection of popular culture with mass media in the daily lives of audiences and ethnographies of how this intersection informs their sense of self and culture will provide a rich understanding of how global interacts with local.
>
> (McMillin 2007: 192)

NEW MEDIA?

We compared the 'change acceleration' of the 20th century to what came before and viewed it as incomparable. But the changes to media from the mid-1990s to 2011 (just over 15 years) could reasonably be considered as significant as the advent of mass literacy, but taking hundreds of years less to impact on the fabric of our lives. **Web 2.0** has become a shared label for the point at which the internet became more like Tim Berners-Lee (its inventor) imagined it to be – a place where we can share, participate, create and interact. So the idea is that Web 1.0 was a 'push down' internet, defined, like the rest of mass media, by elite producers providing content for audiences (web browsers) but now Web 2.0 allows us to make the media for ourselves – a media landscape defined by horizontal connection rather than vertical 'delivery' – although we will see later on that it's a little more complicated than this when we look at how content is filtered.

Every year, *Time* Magazine – produced in America but sold all over the world – names an individual as 'person of the year' for their contribution to the human race. In 2006, its chosen person was 'you' – all of us, for our collaborative role in the development of 'the age of information'.

This is the point (at the start of this century) where Media Studies started to get confused and its this state of complexity that we encounter here in this introduction to the subject. To put it crudely, this book would have been a lot more straightforward ten years ago, but the good news is that it's a lot more interesting now. Ten years ago, we would have analysed different media sectors in relative isolation from one another – film, TV, news, even videogames. We would have looked at theories of mass audiences and of ideology – how 'big media' influence us in ways that we might see as political or corporate. Now, it's not so easy to say where one media ends and another begins, or where the producers end and the consumers begin.

This state of confusion is all down to **convergence**. Media Studies' first response was to separate the Internet from the traditional concepts and content of the curriculum, so students might take a unit or module in 'New Media' or 'Online Media'. New Media is still a term that you will find in the titles of books and courses, and in the context of this long history we could still use the label with some credibility. But in the lifespan of the majority of Media students, there is nothing 'new' about the Internet. Gauntlett argues that:

> The view of the Internet and new digital media as an 'optional extra' is replaced with recognition that they have fundamentally changed the ways in which we engage with all media.
>
> (Gauntlett 2007: 2)

If so, then the study of contemporary Media is the study of the Internet. But does that mean that every YouTube upload, every blog or even every tweet can be studied within the curriculum? Or is it only 'mass media', in its online form, that counts? Are virtual worlds 'media texts' or just places – no more a media product than your own town or city? Media Studies hasn't really decided what to do about these questions at the moment, so perhaps a part of your job as a student of media will be to work out some of the answers.

There are, or course, 'lighter' and 'heavier' things to study in the world of '**Media Studies 2.0**', On the one hand, the question we have just posed – do the many versions of *Dramatic Cat* on YouTube count as media texts worthy of academic study, alongside *The Social Network*? But on the other, there is the function of social media in Iran, Tunisia and Egypt where citizens were able to organize and protest with hitherto impossible levels of organization through the affordances of Twitter. The balance of power shifts – but to what extent?

Crucially, it should always be in your mind that studying Media is about questions of culture, not of technology. Education tends to try to neatly categorize and separate these things – so English students look at poetry, Media students look at videogames and IT students know about technology. But how people use technology to respond to, and create, texts is a cultural issue. The starkest warning against 'technological determinism' (whereby we end up over-celebrating IT developments without applying sufficient criticality to their role in culture) comes from de la Feunte:

> In a perverse irony, cultural studies academics and sociologists who study media have come to mirror the techniques used by those they have often been keen to differentiate themselves from – namely, experts in marketing and consumer research.
>
> (de le Fuente 2011: 40)

HOW TO STUDY MEDIA

Academic courses related to media generally adopt a series of key conceptual approaches. These might be more or less practically applied and each teaching department will have its theoretical preferences, but generally speaking the toolkit you will need – and which we will make use of throughout this book – contains the following instruments of analysis:

TEXTUAL DECONSTRUCTION

> At its simplest level media literacy is the ability to use a range of media and be able to understand the information received. At a more advanced level it moves from recognising and comprehending information to the higher order critical thinking skills such as questioning, analysing and evaluating that information. This aspect of media literacy is sometimes referred to as 'critical viewing' or 'critical analysis'.
>
> (OFCOM statement, 2007)

The form of a media text is its shape and structure and the combination of the 'micro' elements such as, for radio, dialogue, music and atmospheric sound, effects, editing and ambience. The form of a text is instantly recognizable to the audience – for example, soap opera, a third person shooter videogame, newspaper, historical film drama. The style of a text is the way the text uses the form. Studying media texts (sometimes neatly separated from each other, like films and TV shows, and sometimes – and increasingly – intertextually connected to other texts online and thus *converged*) and pulling them apart to see how they have been put together to make meaning in relation to *genre* (types and categories of texts with sets of conventions that make them recognizable to audiences); *narrative* (ways of telling stories through editing and implication) and *representation* (how media texts relate to our ideas of the 'real world' by (re)presenting reality in various ways). Conventions are usually described as the 'ingredients' of a particular form or genre. For example, there are 'rules of engagement' for news broadcasts and the way games are marketed share a range of conventions with Hollywood film franchises. Another example is period drama, a subgenre with a range of necessary ingredients, which are expected by the audience, making conventions 'contractual' in nature.

AUDIENCE THEORIES

> Arguably, audience research has always revolved around issues of power. Either we want to know what the media do to people, what people do to media, or perhaps, what people do to themselves and others *with* media.
>
> (Ruddock 2007: 25)

These have developed, over time, from models of passive audiences 'receiving' messages from media to more active '**reception**' theories through to the more contemporary and 'postmodern' schools of thought that see the idea of 'the audience' itself as problematic – 'the concept formally known as the audience', even. The relationship between generalized models of audience behaviour and actual evidence from sustained research is important and the best way for media students to engage with audience theories is always to undertake their own audience research.

THEORIES OF IDEOLOGY

> Hegemony is the ability of the ruling classes to rule by consent, by evolving a consensus for the ruling sentiments through everyday cultural life, including media representation of the world.
>
> (Sardar and Van Loon 2000: 72)

These are those 'macro' approaches to the long-term 'cultivating' impact of media on how we see the world and each other, from the mediating influence of body image cultivation and its potential link to eating disorders in children to the more 'Big P' political influence (such as Murdoch's power over politicians, challenged for the first time in decades in the UK as a result of phone-hacking revelations) analysed by Chomsky and including less measurable issues around what we come to view as 'normal' and 'deviant'. Studying media always includes this socio-political dimension and questions of democracy, ownership and power as well as the degree to which we can resist and rework the mainstream circulation of media meaning through things like fan activity, 'remix culture' and citizen media.

THEORIES OF IDENTITY

> A focus on identity requires us to pay close attention to the diverse ways in which media and technologies are used in everyday life, and their consequences both for individuals and for social groups.
>
> (Buckingham 2008: 19)

We started this book by situating Media Studies as 'everyday', stating that our daily lives are mediated. If that's true, then how can we say where our identities and media begin and end? Media do not solely determine our identities, of course, but they play a role and various academic ways of studying how humans negotiate identities offer important methods for connecting media to the broader tapestry of individual, local, collective, national and global culture. In addition, more recent theories and research interventions are exploring the possibilities for anonymous activity and 'playful' subversion of identity in online spaces and virtual worlds, so this area is becoming ever more important in studying media – but also more complex.

THEORIES OF CREATIVITY

> The web has enabled people to cast off the primarily slumped, passive model of twentieth century 'leisure time', and given them the opportunity to embrace a more social and connected life of creative exchange.
>
> (Gauntlett 2011a: 237)

Most of the time, studying media involves making media, and after all you don't need to be a media academic these days to do this. Theories that look at what being creative actually means are becoming more useful in Media Studies. If we produce our own versions of media texts but stay faithful to the conventions of 'real media', is this creative or just imitation? Or is all imitation an act of parody which is always creative, a reworking of a template and its meanings? As **'prosumers'** increasingly make their own media, do we still need professionals to teach us the 'craft' of making interesting work in any medium (or across converged **'transmedia'** spaces)? And what is the relationship between media, commerce and art?

For media students, the important skills to develop here are being critically reflective (situating your own creative work in the contexts of identity and conceptions of audience) and being able to 'theorize' your own creativity – applying the conceptual toolkit outlined above to your own material.

WHO ARE MEDIA?

This is the most factual and (potentially) straightforward area of Media Studies – you need to know which companies and corporations produce the media we consume and who owns those companies. The complex element of this is taking an informed position on the political and economic debates around these facts.

Web 2.0 has made it a lot more difficult to pin down the relationship between ownership of media and influence on society than it used to be, in the days before people could make their own media or interact more tangibly online with media. So we are left with a contradiction – as we might expect a breakdown of the dominant corporations, as 'we media' takes over, we have actually seen an increased concentration of ownership and it is certainly the case that the most seemingly 'democratic' Web 2.0 platforms are in many cases owned by the same huge conglomerates that had a stronghold over 'old media' and the ownership patterns of broadcast and print media stay the same.

MEDIA ECONOMICS

There is a clear relationship between media economics and media power. While the internet (and Web 2.0 in particular) has transformed the media environment so that the user can become the producer and content can be organically developed and shared, it is still the case that concentrated ownership ensures that the money for media comes from, and is returned to, with profits, a small cluster of super-powerful companies. These include Microsoft, Google, Time Warner, Disney and News Corporation – each of these has a market share of between $50 billion and $150 billion. The importance of conglomerate economics is another crucial factor because it complicates matters in an important way. For example, all of the major Hollywood studios also own companies producing and distributing television, music, newspapers, publishing and games. And the Internet has, despite all the hype around its 'we media' potential, followed the same pattern:

> With a few exceptions, there is little debate that a shrinking number of corporations control more and more of the firms producing media content and the firms that own the conduits through which that content flows. ... While there may well be an almost infinite number of sites on the internet, it turns out that virtually all of those who seek out information use a very small number of sites, most of which are owned by very large media corporations.
>
> (Press and Williams 2010: 41)

This is a different kind of ownership and control, though. It is control by filter in a media landscape characterized by an abundance of information and content, whereas in the linear age, control was achieved by being the main provider in a landscape of scarcity. So the contemporary media environment is about a proliferation of choice and content – some of which we produce for ourselves, but it is also defined by tight concentration of how we filter this content.

Here we are generalizing and studying media involves awareness of norms and exceptions, generalizations and inconsistencies. For example, Hollywood dominates world cinema – and this situation is analysed by media theorists as a state of cultural imperialism, but at the same time we can see that **diaspora** (the dispersal of people and their cultures across the world) ensures that Bollywood is a strong rival – a similar industry in scale and economics but with a very different audience structure – Indian communities dispersed around the globe wanting to connect to their 'heritage' culture, as opposed to the 'glocalization' of Hollywood all over the world. In addition, there are countries where media is overtly state-controlled, but again there are great differences in how this is managed. The Chinese government is constantly attempting to censor media but recently their relationship with Google has been stretched due to this. In the UK, the BBC operates as a public service broadcaster and a mistake many Media students make when first researching it is to think it is state-controlled. In fact, UK tax-payers own the BBC and that makes it 'super-independent' of government but the regulation of the BBC is an area where UK governments attempt greater or lesser control, depending on their political agenda (whether they want more or less control of media or whether they want more or less competition for other companies to challenge the BBC). In communist Cuba, connections to the outside (capitalist) world have traditionally been greatly restricted but the Cuban government has actively harnessed new media technology for economic developments internally and, since Fidel Castro's health declined, he has used the internet instead of TV and radio broadcasting to communicate to the Cuban population. However, there is a (perhaps technologically determinist) view that the Internet will, ultimately, break down state control in Cuba, but this warning from Venegas should warn us to guard against such a complacent view in any context:

> In no way does access to the Internet equate with a potential for democracy. The determinist assumption behind such an equation assumes that access to more information and new tools to promote individual action leads to the creation of politicized communities able and willing to oppose hegemonic political and economic structures. Prescribing this logic for Cuba fails to consider inherent economic limitations (such as low wages and expensive hardware) that prevent the majority of the population from even owning a computer.
>
> (Venegas 2010: 93)

So we can see that a successful student of media must be careful to avoid such prescription – assuming a worldview from a Western, developed nation perspective and seeing change and transformation as being consistent across borders. At the same time, it is true that patterns of power – the relationship between ownership, control, regulation, information and expression are changing, and that technology is playing a big part in that, albeit hugely staggered 'revolution'.

THE FUTURE

In 2011, a range of academics, researchers and teachers joined forces to create a 'Manifesto for Media Education' (Fraser and Wardle 2011) to look ahead to the future and describe the directions that Media Studies might follow. Here are a selection of the statements and suggestions, appearing simply in alphabetical order, followed by

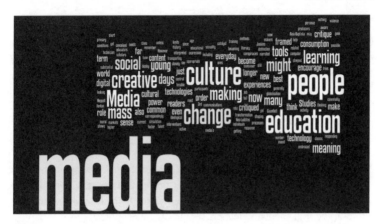

Figure 1.1 A Media Studies Cloud

some synthesis of the common themes – the elements that appear in bold type are those we are drawing out for our overview:

There is little doubt about **the central role of the media** – and of consumer culture more broadly – in the continuing transformation of modern societies.

(Buckingham)

The point of media education is to critique **power** and the power of meaning making.

(Fenton)

Ultimately, Media Studies should encourage **creative thinking and creative making**. Media Studies should give people the tools – or help them to invent the tools – which will foster creative exchange between individuals and groups.

(Gauntlett)

Media Education has the potential to be a **disruptive catalyst** transporting learning into the 3rd millennium.

(Heppell)

Media education needs to be framed for **participants**, a role distinct from yet closely related to both producers and consumers as they were classically conceived.

(Jenkins)

The **critique of technology**, which should be a primary job of media educators, is generally assumed to be the territory of so-called Neo-Luddites. It's possible to be a media user and a **critic** simultaneously.

(Lopez)

In an age of user-generated content, visual methods and **cultural convergence,** Media teachers need to get their geek on.

(Potamitis)

Education should be, fundamentally, philosophical, by which I mean driven by questions about knowledge, power and being. Given that the media are constitutive of knowledge, power and being it seems reasonable to argue that media education should be **philosophical.**

(Readman)

Media education processes may really become important in order to achieve a higher order of **media literacy**, both for media readers and media makers.

(Reia-Baptista)

Instead of pushing media education as if it were a discipline, I look for opportunities to integrate multiple literacies into **broader design elements** like problem-solving, experiential learning, collaborative learning, scenarios, simulations, models and interdisciplinary learning.

(Tyner)

Media courses for many students offer **pleasure and enjoyment of learning,** and we would argue that there is nothing inherently wrong with that!

(Wardle)

Viewing the tag cloud derived from these future-gazing projections, it's clear that there remains a strong belief that Media Studies is more of a catalyst for changing people – and then, by stealth, changing society – than other academic subjects would claim to be. The prominence of the word 'change' indicates both that the contributors are in agreement that media is changing but equally that studying media can change the dynamics between powerful media and people in a democracy. If there any doubt about the status of Media Studies as a humanities discipline (and for some, it should be thought of as interdisciplinary), the significance of 'people' would suggest that engaging with it takes students beyond a mere vocational training in skills and competences. Other words looming large are 'culture', 'creative' and 'social', again rooting the subject in the study of the everyday, but with a new focus on how people are creative producers of their own media or at least creative respondents to 'real media'. The disagreements are over the degree to which we should see these changes as determined by technology and with that the extent to which technical advances/affordances should necessarily be celebrated and also the degree to which everyday creativity is more significant than the practices of powerful media corporations. Perhaps Cary Bazalgette's contribution is the most helpful to an introductory book such as this, so we shall take it as an 'agenda' for what follows, and for your engagements with Media Studies in the future:

> Is it all about challenging the **high culture-popular culture** divide? Is it all about **protecting** young people from, or arming them against, the media's endemic violence, sexuality, moral turpitude, cultural superficiality or ideological conspiracies? Is it more about vocational **training** to encourage talent and sustain our **creative industries**? Or is it now just all about getting on top of the new **digital technologies** and learning how to use them effectively? My response here is to ask: why shouldn't media education do all of these?
>
> (C. Bazalgette in Fraser and Wardle, 2011)

SUMMARY

This chapter has introduced you to the idea that 'media' is a broad term to describe a range of texts and activities. We have explored the debates around media and their importance to people and in society and we have traced a history of communication, media and technology and, alongside this, a history of methods for studying media. Finally, we have looked to the future to anticipate where the study of media might take us in the next few years. The ideas and examples covered in this chapter can lead to the following summative statements:

* Media Studies is carried out and interpreted in response to a range of discursive ideas about media, people in everyday life

and ideas about society, power and democracy. It's complicated, and people don't agree about it.

* Digital technologies have played, and are playing, a transformative role in the relationship between people and media. This will continue and accelerate, so Media Studies is going to change, and will keep changing.

* Despite this pace of change, there are some stable theoretical concepts that have been in place since Media Studies began and, while these will have to adapt, they are likely to survive in the future and they are genre, narrative, representation, ideology and audience.

* Also despite great changes in media choice and access, it is still the case that a small number of big multinational corporations dominate media ownership and so students of media need to analyse what this means in terms of power, information and influence in contemporary society. At the time of writing, this equation was more prominent in public discourse than ever before, in the wake of the News Corporation phone-hacking scandal, so the study of media and power is far from an outdated area.

* Theories of creativity are becoming more important to students of media as more and more ordinary people start to make their own media.

* Being a student of media always involves making media, but the critical perspectives are the same whether we are analysing 'real' media or our own creative work – these are questions of power, representation, identity (local, national, global) and meaning-making. For these we need high levels of *critical* media literacy.

FURTHER READING

All of the work referred to in this chapter is listed in the bibliography at the end of the book, but the key recommended reading on the material covered in this chapter is as follows:

Buckingham, D. (ed) (2008) *Youth, Identity and Digital Media*. Cambridge, MA: MIT Press.
A collection of research-based articles exploring the role of digital media in the lives of young people and its role in forming identities.

Chomsky, N. (2002) *Media Control: The Spectacular Achievements of Propaganda*. New York: Seven Stories.
An introduction to Chomsky's classic theory of how media 'manufacture consent'.

de Zengotita, T. (2005) *Mediated: How the Media Shape Your World*. London: Bloomsbury.
The theory of 'mediation' is important to contemporary Media Studies.

Fraser, P. and Wardle, J. (2011) *A Manifesto for Media Education*, www.mani festoformediaeducation.co.uk.
Prominent Media Studies teachers and academics looking to the future of the subject.

Press, A. and Williams, B. (2010) *The New Media Environment: An Introduction*. Oxford: Wiley-Blackwell.
Applies a range of media theories to the specific, changing nature of 21st century media.

2

READING MEDIA
DOING TEXTUAL ANALYSIS

AIMS

This chapter will introduce you to:

* 'Micro' textual analysis for still images
* 'Micro' textual analysis for moving images;
* Approaches to critical media literacy for time and space based texts;
* New conceptual models for deconstructing contemporary media forms.

'Micro' textual analysis refers to the study of specific elements of media texts that can be deconstructed only through the act of 'close reading'. While there is a great deal of crossover, for the purposes of introducing this practice, still images are usually considered first, before moving on to moving image analysis. Then, the 'micro' features of texts are assessed in a thematic way to relate them to broader 'macro' conceptual models of media analysis.

MEDIA LANGUAGE: STILL IMAGE ANALYSIS

Media language describes the combination of written, verbal, non-verbal, aural and aesthetic communication and its instantaneous connection to meaning. The task of the critically media literate student is simply to '**deconstruct**' this assemblage of meaning. Generally, media courses begin with still images and work on to moving images, so for this reason this chapter follows suit. Still image analysis often begins with semiotics – the study of signs.

Semiotics is a branch of Structuralism and notable figures in this theoretical school include Peirce, Saussure and Barthes. Structuralism sought to identify structures that provide a network for meaning as located in texts (stories, images, clothes, films, videogames, dance movements – anything that carries meaning beyond its physical properties). The focus here is on how meaning is constructed within a culture in a systematic way. Semiotics looks at meaning at the level of the individual sign, which is divided into its signifier and its signified. If the sign is a man's tie, then the signifier is the physical property that we can all agree on (a garment around a man's neck with a particular texture and colour) and the signified is what meaning we attribute to it – this is conceptual – we imagine it, or at least agree on what it 'means' without there being a 'natural' logical reason why it should mean this. So, there is an agreement that a man ought to wear a tie in certain situations – certain forms of work or business, often at a wedding, certainly for most people at a job interview. But why? The signified is to do with formality, being 'smart', appropriate attire, taking thing seriously. But the signifier doesn't in itself dictate that. It is a cultural decision.

Our names are signs, as are all words. Once we learn a language, we cannot stop to disconnect the signifier from the signified. When we are in a foreign country where we cannot understand the language, we just hear the sounds, but once we know the language we are constantly and instantaneously decoding the meaning of every sign. Here is an illustration:

Read these words (they are in Lithuanian) – *braškių ir šalto alaus*. A minority of readers may be, or may speak, Lithuanian but the chances are that most readers have no idea what these signs (letters, combined together in words) mean. In English, they translate as 'strawberries and cold beer'. When you are looking at this second set of signifiers, you can't help but attach the signified – you are thinking of the fruit and the beverage and its temperature. This is how signs work, the signified is instantly attached. But this is only the first level of *signification*, of course. Next, personal life experience, values and taste come in to add a level of *connotation*. Perhaps it is the time of day when a cold beer appeals. Or perhaps you are allergic to strawberries. These things mean that the signified is not fixed for everyone.

Media texts are combinations of lots of signs. Creators of texts make decisions about settings, objects, costume, appearance, dialogue, sound, lighting – all of these are signifiers. According to the 'science' of semiotics, there are three kinds of signs:

ICONIC SIGNS

These have a direct resemblance to what they represent in the 'real world' – for example, a photograph of a celebrity or somebody you know. Or a painting of a church that really exists.

SYMBOLIC SIGNS

These have a completely arbitrary, or 'made up' cultural connection to what they represent – once we agree on the meaning, we accept it but if we wanted to we could change it. For example, a 'no entry' road sign doesn't have to look the way it does. Equally, the word 'zoo' could be exchanged for the word 'chair'. *Come in and pull up a zoo. We're all going to the chair tomorrow.* It sounds crazy, for sure, but if we just agreed to swap them around, it wouldn't matter because they are just symbols for the concepts they signify – a four legged structure to sit on or a collection of animals kept in custody to entertain and educate humans.

INDEXICAL SIGNS

These have some kind of indirect or suggestive relationship to what they represent – for example a 'no smoking' sign which does feature a 'referent' of/to a cigarette but the red line that is across it does not really appear in the physical world when a smoker lights up in an 'illegal' space. But the red line suggests 'crossing out' so this kind of sign is not as purely symbolic or as arbitrary as the no entry sign example.

The richest example for discussion is the cross symbol from Christianity. To a Christian who takes the Bible literally, this will

Figure 2.1 Ned at the Nou Camp

be iconic. To an atheist, it's symbolic. To another kind of Christian, it's either more or less symbolic or more or less indexical depending on the extent to which the crucifixion is taken as a historical event and the extent to which it is symbolic of a set of ideas about faith.

To show how far we can take semiotics when looking at just one still image, let's consider this image of a five-year-old boy at the Nou Camp stadium, Barcelona.

If we pose the following questions, the answers will all be semiotic in the sense that they will make sense but only within the structure of signification – i.e. what we have agreed, culturally, that things have come to 'mean' at the level of what Barthes calls 'myth'.

QUESTION: WHY TAKE A PHOTOGRAPH IN FRONT OF THIS SIGN?

Answer: Barthes (1984) writes a lot about the idea of the photograph as memory or attempt to preserve a moment and there are all kinds of signification wrapped up in this. Clearly this is a trip to a stadium that requires recording as a special occasion. For the football supporter, Barcelona in 2011 has a special status as arguably the best club team to have ever played their sport. For English football supporters, they are the exotic 'other' – the way they pass the ball and play the 'beautiful game' is completely at odds with the 'high octane' kick and rush version produced by the Premier League and the English national team. So wrapped up in this image is the sense of a pilgrimage to a 'Mecca' of the sport, to pay respects. One useful strategy we can use to understand semiotics better is the 'commutation test' where we simply swap elements to see what difference it makes. A photograph taken in front of Meadow Lane, the home of Notts County football club will have a very different set of meanings – Notts County are the oldest league club so, for sure, there will be history, but the East Midlands setting is profoundly unglamorous and the trophy cabinet is bare, so these two sets of 11 football players have entirely different cultural meanings despite the fact that in the end they both get paid to kick a ball around. These contrasts are all at the level of the signified.

QUESTION: WHY DOES A BOY FROM BIRMINGHAM WANT TO WEAR THE BARCELONA KIT?

Answer: Partly as a holiday souvenir but also because of the connotations the kit carries – skill, winning trophies, glamour, very expensive players. The sponsor, UNESCO, also sets up Barcelona as a more global brand.

QUESTION: WHAT'S THE MEANING OF THE HAT?

Answer: This is a hat from Cuba, signifying the revolution (see the case study in Chapter 4). As Cuba is Spanish-speaking (but not Catalan, the home language of Barcelona), there are some complex cultural connections. Catalan identity is unique and the football club signifies these meanings in addition to those we have outlined already. Furthermore, a young boy from Birmingham wearing a hat bought in Cuba in Barcelona carries meanings about global culture and postmodern signification (see Chapter 4).

QUESTION: WHAT'S THE MEANING OF '*MÉS QUE UN CLUB*'?

Answer: This is Barcelona's motto and it carries connotations of Catalan identity that set the club apart from the rest of Spain and the world. This is where football partisanship takes on another symbolic level. Just as Celtic versus Rangers 'means' more in Glasgow, Scotland, than just a football match when it is associated with Catholic and Protestant belief systems and politics (Celtic are a Catholic club and Rangers are Protestant and for a long time a sectarian policy determined who could play for each team), there is a shared cultural view (a 'myth' in Barthes' terms) that Barcelona and Real Madrid represent competing sides in Spanish politics and the struggle against fascism. On one level, of course, this is nonsense – the players are from all over the world and will have little sense of this history, the supporters live in a very different contemporary Spain and many of their followers are from overseas (like Manchester United, Barcelona is very much a 'global brand'). This mindset is dangerous and certainly not to be encouraged. In both Spain and Scotland, death threats are common when these 'local derbies' are held. But these subcultural tensions are somehow given longevity in the form of football matches. Now, the five-year-old boy in the photograph won't appreciate any of this but he *will* understand the global meaning of 'Barca' as 'more than a club' when compared to, say, Plymouth Argyle. This means that we can use one of the most (arguably) pretentious Media Studies terms here to say that, like *The Simpsons*, the meanings of Barcelona football club are 'multilayered'.

This is merely a contemporary application of Barthes' influential semiotic analysis of *Mythologies* (1984). We're doing the same thing here that Barthes did with steak and chips:

> Steak is in France a basic element, nationalized even more than socialized. It figures in all the surroundings of elementary life – flat, edged with yellow, like the sole of a shoe, in cheap restaurants; thick and juicy in

the bistros which specialize in it, cubic: with the core all moist throughout beneath a light charred crust, in haute cuisine. It is a part of all the rhythms, that of the comfortable bourgeois meal and that of the bachelor's bohemian snack. It is food at once expeditious and dense, it effects the best possible ratio between economy and efficacy, between mythology and its multifarious ways of being consumed.

(Barthes 1984: 70)

To 'get' the idea of mythology, critical media students need to avoid the temptation to observe that 'it's just food'. Semiotics helps us to look at what things represent symbolically – beyond what they 'are in themselves' – but only if we let them, only if we agree on their connotations in a coherent system of **discourse** and **myth** – not 'myth' in the sense of a lie, of course (and very importantly) but 'myth' as abstracted symbolic consensus.

MEDIA LANGUAGE: MOVING IMAGE ANALYSIS

Firstly, it's an obvious point, but moving images are still images moving. This is important to state because it reminds us that everything covered in the previous section applies to moving images as well, with the key additions of sound and editing. When deconstructing moving image texts, the key elements are *camera* (position, angle, movement, framing, lens choice), *editing* (in some ways the most important and fundamental aspect of meaning-making), *sound* (diegetic – in the world of the text and non-diegetic – added for the audience only) and *mise en scène* (this describes the overall atmosphere and sense of time and place created by such things as lighting, costume, setting and effects in combination to, as the French term describes, 'put into the scene').

Taking each in turn, these are the key questions a critical media student will ask in order to develop an advanced level of critical media literacy.

CAMERA

In what ways does the *choice of shot* situate the viewer to convey meaning? What meanings are set up by a long shot and a 'point of view' (POV) shot? If used as an establishing shot, then a long shot shows the viewer where they are in the scene. A POV makes us feel as though we are part of the scene – these types of camera choice situate us as spectators/viewers. *Angles* add to meaning – a high POV shot suggests superiority, while a low-angle POV shot conveys weakness. *Camera movement* adds another layer – a zoom can highlight emotion on a character, jerky hand-held POV shots can provide tension and convey a sense of involvement in action sequences. *Focus* is used to highlight important elements in the narrative/storyline. Of course, these are things we don't think about too much when 'just watching'. In fact, 'just watching' is difficult to avoid when studying media. But the reason why these things appear to be commonplace and even a 'natural' way for moving images to tell stories, is because we have come to accept them over time as conventional, so understanding the **conventions** of media texts and the degree to which, at the 'micro' level, particular texts reinforce or challenge/subvert conventions is a fundamental part of close reading.

EDITING

This is the hardest part of close reading, precisely because editing is often intended to seem 'invisible' and the fact that we don't notice it is, again, due to its conventional nature. Put simply, the meaning of moving images often resides in the connections and relations between shots, rather than in separate shots themselves. Editing helps to convey meaning through the manipulation of time and space. We can see two storylines at once, we can jump forward in time or do the opposite through flashbacks. Obvious points, but editing is often a matter of doing what is impossible in 'real life' but making it appear real. Jump cuts, cross-cuts and cutaways are used to add more symbolic meaning rather than just tell a story more quickly or without boring the audience. Further symbolic layers are added by making choices about *rhythm* and *pace* – fast-paced/frequent cuts convey action, while slow-paced/infrequent cuts convey unfolding drama or perhaps romance. *Persuasion* is critical here, the *'grammar of the edit'* has the intention of trying to influence our view of the sequence of events and what they mean. *Ellipsis* describes the process of removing parts of the story (narrative) and this can be more or less explicit or implicit. **Dialectical** montage (from the Soviet director, Eisenstein) is an academic term to describe the simple, everyday process of combining two shots to construct meaning. But it only seems so simple and everyday because it is so conventional – everyone does it, we expect it, it is 'the way things are'. The critical media student must always look at the edit and ask, how is it trying to persuade?

SOUND

The combination of sound and image adds a number of layers to meaning. Sound provides **anchorage**, it pins down the meaning, for example, romantic music as a soundtrack to two people staring into each other's eyes tells you that you are watching a romantic scene. Horror, comedy, action, news, documentary all have their conventional kinds of music that seem appropriate and in turn tell us how we should be feeling. Again, these only seem 'natural' because we have come to accept them over time. Sound provides either *contrast* or *flow* – it can provide an indication as to whether the direction of a story is changing or staying the same. **Diegetic** sound describes sound that originates from within the narrative (the world of the text). For example, the sound from a CD that we hear when an actor presses play. Non-diegetic sound is sound that is not part of the narrative – such as background music – that is added just for the audience, to help convey meaning. Sometimes we find examples that are both or neither, consider a voiceover of a character's thoughts for instance.

MISE EN SCÈNE

This academic term refers to the overall atmosphere/ambience of a scene (everything in front of the camera). It is achieved through a combination of elements: costume, lighting, props, sound and the performance of actors (as well as the casting).

These micro elements 'add up' to the construction of **verisimilitude** – a logical sense of '**realism**' that we accept when viewing a moving image text. It doesn't necessarily mean 'realistic'. Instead it describes a state of 'believable' textual reality. For example, when we are watching *Lord of the Rings*, we don't believe that it mirrors our experience of reality, but nevertheless it has a logical textual world that we understand and this means that if a hobbit carried an iPhone, it would break the 'realism'. This is generic realism – it adopts the conventions for the genre that we have come to accept. Cultural, or social realism, is that which attempts to convince us that it is an authentic representation of the existing social world, whether fictional or not.

In summary, all of these individual micro elements such as camera angles, editing, sound and elements of *mise en scène* add up to a set of meanings that we can apply 'macro' theories to understand. But – and this is vital – we must always remember that the active audience makes the meaning (based on cultural experiences and literacy practices). There are always a range of ways in which elements of a text may be interpreted, this plurality of meaning is called **polysemy**.

CASE STUDY: *SUPERSIZE ME*

This documentary film (2004) chronicles a research project undertaken by its director, Morgan Spurlock, in which he eats only food from McDonald's for 30 days. In one early scene, we see and hear him ordering from a 'drive-thru', eating a supersize quarter pounder with cheese meal (with fries and coke), suffering from the effects of such a large quantity of fast food and then vomiting out of the driver's window.

Except that we don't.

What we see and hear is a much briefer edited version of these events. At several times we are given elliptical information on screen (such as '15 minutes later'). What we actually witness is about four mouthfuls and some slow chewing. To be graphic, we don't even really see him being sick – we see him about to be sick and then the camera tilts down to the pavement where we see a pile of vomit. What we do, then, as readers of this media text, is not only accept the edit, but even add to the story for the producers – we imagine that he has eaten the full meal in between the shots we are treated to, and we accept that it's his vomit on the floor. Now, a critical deconstruction of the text doesn't mean we are saying it isn't true, that he didn't eat the full meal or that he wasn't unwell as a result. Instead, it's a critical understanding of the way that the edit constructs a particular version of events. Clearly, the intention of the documentary is to cast McDonald's in a pretty bad light and this is a powerful scene in so doing – a healthy man just isn't capable of eating a supersize meal at the start of the project, just as a healthy person would be ill the first time they took heroin. But whether or not the scene is 'accurate' is a different question, the critical media student's role is to deconstruct the edit and the 'preferred reading' as the producer intends it.

FILM STUDIES

Film Studies and Media Studies are separate academic fields (though clearly interrelated) and there is an excellent 'Basics' title by Villarejo (2007) from which this statement is helpful:

> Cinema's dynamism, its capacity to arrange and rearrange time and motion, thus reveals its dimensions that are deeply social, historical, industrial, technological, philosophical, political, aesthetic, psychological, personal and so forth. The aggregate of these multiple dimensions indeed *is* cinema.
>
> (Villarejo 2007: 9)

Here we are in the realm of the 'macro'. Villarejo is describing what the 'micro' close readings of film texts will add up to in terms of how we can analyse films in relation to life and society. There are some 'bridging' theories which are specific to Film Studies that are usually encountered by students of Media as well.

GENRE, AUTEUR, STAR, SPECTATORSHIP

SPECTATORSHIP

This describes more than just watching films. It's to do with how we receive films in the contexts of our social and political lives, how we attribute value to some films and not others, and why. Films are analysed as products with four life stages – *production*, *distribution*, *exhibition* and *reception*. The latter is not an isolated phase, so theories of spectatorship look at ways in which the way we view films is institutionalized, generic and informed by marketing and promotion. So the relationship between production and reception is a 'fluid exchange' (Villarejo 2007: 128).

GENRE

Genre is perhaps the most 'classic' of Media Studies' key concepts. A genre is a category of media text that comes to be recognizable through its **conventions**. From then on, a circular contract is in place between producers and audiences, based on a series of expectations and gratifications and a developing progression whereby the conventions are added to, built on, challenged, subverted and reworked or remediated in different formats. Branston and Stafford sum this up here:

> Genres are seen no longer as sets of fixed elements, constantly repeated and occasionally innovated within, but as working with 'repertoires of elements', fluid systems of learnt conventions and expectations. These are shared by makers and audiences, who are both active on both sides of meaning-making. The maker can rely on certain kinds of audience familiarity to play with, and the audience looks forward to play within these stabilities.

(Branston and Stafford 2010: 83)

CASE STUDY: A GENRE MAP

The study of genre often starts with more rudimentary 'convention spotting' and a consideration of the interplay between and across genres. For example, for television genres, one easy way of starting to think more sharply about conventions is to draw a 'tube map'. The idea is to build up a network of TV dramas along the same lines as the London Tube Map and its creative variations, taking the idea from Dorian Lynskey's underground map of 100 years of music history (at http://blogs.guardian.co.uk/culturevulture/archives/2006/02/03/post_51.html).

This is done by simply listing all the names of all the TV dramas you are aware of, past and present, on individual Post-It notes. It can be more straightforward if you start by looking at a single genre, such as crime drama. Then you start to think about how all these various programmes can be categorized in different ways – by genre, format, decade, potential audience, region, gender, ethnic groups, star, production company and any other criteria you can add to the mix. You can equally well categorize according to typical conventions – for example police team/individual detective; urban/rural. Next, the job is to arrange the texts into a wide variety of 'routes' – for example, women detectives (*Prime Suspect*), forensic investigations (*CSI*, *Silent Witness*), undercover cops (*The Wire*), urban realism (*The Wire*, *The Bill*, *Prime Suspect* again). On the other hand, if you avoid limiting the texts within a single genre, you can have alternative 'routes' such as HBO productions (*The Wire*, *Deadwood*), historical re-enactments (*Deadwood*, *Rome*, *The Pacific*) and even routes based around a single actor. A route for Todd Carty would stretch from *Z Cars* to *The Bill*, via *Grange Hill*, *Tucker's Luck*, *EastEnders*, *Heartbeat* and *Holby City*. Next, it's important to find a number of overlapping areas and hybrid texts that cross over different categories. These can provide a set of 'interchange' stations at which alternative routes merge. Using these interchange texts as the starting point, you can next try to map these 'routes' onto the 'lines' of the underground, demonstrating the various connections between different types and formats of TV drama series. If you compare your outcomes to others, you will find major categorization problems and will come up with very different types of map. This opens up a useful discussion of the problems of genre definition, issues of similarity and difference, intertextuality, and the uses and gratifications of TV drama for different audiences. The complicated nature of genre is at the heart of such an exploration.

So, it is never long before a more straightforward 'listings' approach to genre gives way to an analysis of the more dynamic, complex operations within and between textual categories. Examples are '**postmodern**' reworkings of classic genres that depend upon deep knowledge of the genre on the part of the audience, sometimes parodic (*Come Fly with Me*) and sometimes serious homage (*Gran Torino*) the importance of fan feedback and 'remix' to contemporary genre texts (such as *Dr Who*) and the intertextual 'remediation' of genres into new formats – for instance, *Red Dead Redemption* and *LA Noire* as 'new' format for classic film genres or *Grand Theft Auto 4* as a 'breakthrough' text in the intertextual relationship between high concept genre cinema and video gaming – at once a serious reworking and a pastiche.

AUTEUR THEORY

As the name suggests, this is the part of Media/Film Studies that is closest to English literature in approach to texts. Directors who have produced a range of films with a repertoire of recognizable elements or stylistic traits are granted this status at the point where film reception is informed by the name of the director. Contrasting contemporary examples are Michael Winterbottom, Wong Kar Wai and Andrea Arnold.

MICHAEL WINTERBOTTOM

Many auteurs are synonymous with a genre but Michael Winterbottom is the opposite. *In This World* portrays the hazardous journey made by two refugees en route to London, while *The Road to Guantanamo* fictionalizes the real aftermath of 9/11 and the British/American response, the 'war on terror'. *24 Hour Party People*, its name taken from a song by the Manchester band The Happy Mondays, offers another fictionalized version of 'real life', in this case the rise and fall of Factory Records and the 'Madchester' music scene in the 1980s and early 1990s. The less conventional *9 Songs* and the playful *A Cock and Bull Story* might seem to share little with the more straightforwardly docudrama examples listed here, but what they certainly share is an interest in blurring the boundaries between real events and fiction which is a defining principle of postmodern media. A key example is the beginning of *24 Hour Party People*, when Steve Coogan, playing the part of Factory Records and Granada TV frontman Tony Wilson, turns to the camera, thus breaking the first rule of 'realism' and says: 'You're going to be seeing a lot more of that sort of thing in the film. Although that did actually happen, obviously it's symbolic – it works on both levels.' Winterbottom's films all deliberately mess around with the boundary between 'suspending disbelief', reality and the obviously artificial. In some films this is lighthearted and in others it is anything but, given the subject matter – *The Road to Guantanamo* is an obvious example. *A Cock and Bull Story* is another great example. The film adapts a 'classic' novel by Laurence Sterne but at the same time provides a 'making of' documentary of the construction of the adaptation. *A Cock and Bull Story* takes the idea even further by deliberately 'playing with' the star image of Steve

Coogan, so it is really hard to work out when he is being himself, when he is playing up to the image of Steve Coogan that has been disseminated as a media commodity during his career, when he is rehearsing to be his character and when he is actually playing the character. More recently, Winterbottom took this even further with his television series *The Trip* in which Steve Coogan and Rob Brydon 'played themselves' with great irony and pathos. While *In This World* might appear to be very different – a much more 'serious' film about Afghan refugees – similar techniques are used to 'deconstruct' the film as a text. The actors are real refugees and the film mixes 'real' footage of their journey with scripted scenes. Similarly *The Road to Guantanamo* is a hybrid of documentary and drama, but unlike a conventional docudrama, the rhythm of the film constantly reminds the audience that this 'remixing' of real events is taking place. No attempt is made in any of Winterbottom's film or TV texts to disguise the mixing of styles and the deliberate lack of any one, stable version of 'the real'.

WONG KAR WAI

Wong Kar Wai is also labelled a 'postmodern auteur'. Wong's films – such as *Chungking Express*, *In the Mood for Love* and *Days of Being Wild* – deal with the ways that the context of the changing nature of Hong Kong impacts on people's lives and in particular he pays attention to time, memory and space (between people and between times), more postmodern themes. His characters are often lonely, despite living in an overpopulated, frenetic high-rise cityscape and a key convention of his style is the way he makes characters' lives intersect. He manipulates space and time in unusual ways. Key 'micro examples' are these. In *Chungking Express*, the main male character is referred to only by his police number and the female lead is often accompanied by a sound motif – *California Dreaming* by The Mamas and the Papas. Sometimes she dances along to this song as a diegetic soundtrack, sometimes it plays in the background non-diegetically and sometimes it is not clear which it is – and this confusion is deliberate, an explicit revelation of the constructed nature of the text.

In the Mood for Love is set in an earlier Hong Kong before independence, and features an establishing statement at the start: 'It is a restless moment. Hong Kong, 1962.' The film mixes the historical context with contemporary thematics and explores isolation and the difficulty of 'pinning down' time. Again, both space and time are thus 'played around' with and the viewer is invited to reflect on this 'remixing' of chronology. *Days of Being Wild*, like the two films already discussed here, makes liberal use of popular culture references and music to create a rich layer of intertextual meaning whereby the isolated nature of the characters (often 'anchored' by voiceover) is contrasted with both the location (bustling Hong Kong) and the music (love songs). Irony thus pervades. Wong's avant-garde filmic aesthetic is composed of elliptical storytelling through the use of slow motion, jump cuts and fragmented images.

> Spectators must suspend their beliefs in chronology, time and in many cases, their memories too, in order to fully experience the depth of Wong's evocative filmic creations. Wong's story is continual and the narrative as dependent on the context of the present as of the past. Through Wong's *oeuvre*, Hong Kong becomes a metaphor for the characters and their varied existence. It represents an urban pastiche in which individuals struggle to come to terms with a sense of detachment and loneliness despite the territory's high-density population. Wong's endless array of possible scenarios and the navigation of his protagonists' internal and external journeys in turn constitute an unravelling and reconfiguring of spatio-temporal constrictions.
>
> (Wright 2002: 3)

The critical media student will be most concerned with the instances where the same film can be viewed as an 'auteur film' or as part of a film genre, movement or style.

ANDREA ARNOLD

Andrea Arnold is a British director whose work is sometimes assessed as a unique body of work and sometimes as an example of contemporary 'social realism', as in this example:

> *Red Road* represents one experience of our society, which seems to match Foucault's model – that of a society where the ultimate holders of that power are not visible, or even clearly defined, and where the

exercisers of regulation are able to direct, unseen, the course of the events.

(R. Murray 2008: 40)

Murray is applying Foucault's metaphor of the Panopticon to Arnold's film *Red Road* in relation to the omnipresence of CCTV cameras and how the viewer is situated within a set of representations of representations. Foucault's theory was a metaphor. He took the 'Panopticon' prison design – whereby each prison cell is arranged in a circle around a guard's tower, so that each prisoner believes they are being watched by the guard (whether this is the case or not) and so regulates their own behaviour. Foucault takes this idea of always being watched and applies it to society as a whole, saying that modern societies have replaced direct punishment with constant surveillance. *Red Road* is interesting because it is depicting an aspect of contemporary Britain with both social realist and postmodern stylistics. *Fish Tank*, Arnold's follow up to *Red Road*, shares the interplay of watching/ watcher that drew Murray's Foucaultian interest. Whether we see *Fish Tank* as an Andrea Arnold film, making connections to *Red Road*, or as a social realist film, looking at the representations of the British 'underclass' and council estates as communities that are at once claustrophobic and romantic, depends on the approach we take to film reception, as opposed to anything in the texts themselves. Arnold is very resistant to the idea of 'social realism' and connections that have been made to other 'auteurs' in that field such as Ken Loach:

The thing about the film industry is that it's terribly middle-class, isn't it? All the people who look at it and study it and write about it are middle-class, so they always see films about the working class as being grim, because the people in the film don't have what they have. I very much get the feeling that I am seeing a different place.

(Arnold, interviewed in Mullen 2009: 17)

To complicate matters further, Arnold is also compared to Shane Meadows – an auteur associated both with social realism and also a 'neo-realist' style. Both directors offer a mixture of social realism and more avant-garde and artistic approaches.

So in the case of Arnold, we could look at her films as 'Arnold films' – with the 'Foucaultian' motif of the watcher and the watched – and/or as social realist films and/or as part of a 'new social realism' that is more neo-realist and avant garde (R. Murray 2008).

Another example of how films can be 'read' as auteur, genre or 'movement' films concerns Indian cinema. The study of Bollywood has tended to focus on stars, genre **hybridity** and fandom/spectatorship – a more 'sociological' approach. This is seen as some media analysts as ironic as Indian cinema has, arguably, has a richer vein of auteurs than many other nations (a few examples are Guru Dutt, Raj Kapoor, Mani Ratnam, Mani Kaul, Adoor Gopalakrishnan, Ritwik Ghatak, Priyadarshan, Mira Nair, Nagesh Kukunoor and Kiran Rao). In this case, the desire for Western academics to understand Bollywood/Indian cinema as an alternative to Hollywood and European cinema has, it is suggested, concealed the auteurism of directors in India.

STAR THEORY

Again, it's important to state that it is rarely a case of separating films out into genre films, auteur films, star films. More often than not, a film features stars with identifiable semiotic meanings in their own rights, an auteur director with a repertoire of elements in their *oeuvre* and a set of clear genre expectations that are met or subverted to greater or lesser degrees. So, once again, it's complicated. Star theory is most commonly associated with the work of Richard Dyer (1980) who produced a theory of stars as *commodities* and as cultural signifiers in themselves and in relation to a network of institutional practices. A 'star', then, has a range of meanings that will inform the reception of any film in which they are cast, as a result of an interplay between their personality; image; character roles and off-screen history – this interplay amounts to a con-structed 'persona'. Stardom, understood in this way, is a social phenomenon in which people come to carry meanings way beyond their 'real' labour as actors, they are thus **semiotic**. Since Dyer's intervention, it is argued that celebrity culture has grown hugely:

> The role that stars and celebrities play has expanded and multiplied in recent years. The magnitude of the star flow cannot be escaped: stars are encountered almost everywhere and through different media

networks. In light of this development, it is important to pose two questions. First, how has the 'spectacle of the popular' and its most conspicuous embodiment, the star, functioned at specific historical moments and within given cultures? Second, what are those cultural and social practices that have both contributed and responded to the star expansion?

(Kallioniemi et al. 2007: 1)

REPRESENTATION

This important Media Studies concept is neatly described here by Buckingham:

The notion of 'representation' is one of the founding principles of media education. The media do not offer us a transparent 'window' on the world, but a mediated version of the world. They don't just present reality, they re-present it.

(Buckingham 2003: 57)

Representation is the sum of various 'micro' parts and relates to broader theories of collective identity, cultivation and ideology. Here is an example of how a study of representation might tie together such threads. Looking at media representations of Britain, the theoretical prism would be the ways in which the changing demographics of the UK are negotiated on screen. Within this you might put theory into practice to produce a trailer for a new British film, study new British films (including films such as *Fishtank* and *Somers Town* alongside more commercially prominent examples), television dramas (series such as *Spooks* and *Shameless* and one-off television plays), soap operas, sitcoms (such as *Gavin and Stacey*) and reality/talent TV (looking at changing representations of categories from class, gender, sexuality, age, disability and ethnicity and, in some cases, located within broader contexts of celebrity culture, globalization and capitalism). These areas would cross boundaries sufficiently to develop a deeper theoretical understanding of these areas. One approach to all of this is more quantitative content analysis – how many times are disabled people featured as key characters, what are the stock depictions of ethnicity? More often it will be qualitative and discursive – how do these texts, taken together, form a 'mass' of ideas about reality that are constructed in language?

Ultimately what idea of Britain might be cultivated and then sub-sequently (mis)recognized by these media texts? Linking the 'micro' of semiotics to the 'macro' of representation, what are the 'signifying practices' (Hall 1980) at work here and what broader theories of culture and meaning (Marxism, feminism, theories of identity) might we apply to what we find?

> Meaning is a social production, a practice. The world has to be made to mean. Language and symbolization is the means by which meaning is produced.
>
> (Hall 1980: 67)

Working out how the idea of Britain is 'made to mean' can then lead to contrasting theories of national identity, always a contested arena in Britain. Bragg (2006), in an attempt to reconstruct a pride in Britishness that cannot be tainted as xenophobic, suggests that the hybridity of British identity could be harnessed as a 'value' in itself:

> Establishing space rather than space as our foundation, we can imagine a Britishness which is the sum of every building, field, road, path, every food, custom, belief, culture, every person – in fact, everything that is in Britain today, a Britishness that can only be truly appreciated by under-standing how and why these things came to be here. The British identity is well placed to encompass such diversity.
>
> (Bragg 2006: 281)

Bragg's articulation of a new vision for British identity is con-structed partly as a response to attempts by far-right organizations such as the BNP and the English Defence League to wage war on the 'threat of Islam' by recourse to an ill-defined and confused notion of 'British values' that radical Muslims are perceived to be attacking. In these contexts, the critical media student will make connections between an analysis of contemporary media texts, how they 'make Britain mean' (from Hall) and competing – and confused – notions of British identity (from Bragg).

NARRATIVE

Narrative analysis 'unpacks' the ways that texts organize events into sequences and how these acts of sequencing become conventional.

Over a period of time, these conventional ways of telling stories cross over from one form to another in a process of 'remediation'. The 'classic' formalist theories of narrative that Media Studies draws on come from Propp and Todorov, Soviet theorists who produced morphologies and typologies of how fictional stories tend to deploy a stock of repeated 'character types' and fit a structure that begins with equilibrium and moves through disruption, development, attempts to repair the order of things through conflict and resolution and ultimately a new equilibrium. Classical narrative tends to be based on cause and effect and an underlying structure of meaning that is highly conventional but in no way natural or inevitable. The way that 'the news' is sequenced on television to fit the same format every day, the conventions of sports coverage, our expectation of film trailers and even website navigation protocols are all constructed within a limiting range of structural expectations.

The analysis of 'voice' and how this situates the viewer is important in narrative theory. In one famous example, Martin Scorsese attempts to 'situate' the viewer of *Taxi Driver* in the mindset of a deranged Vietnam veteran working in a New York cab as he spirals towards a horrific killing spree, through the use of a voice over which provides a soundtrack from the mind of Travis Bickle along with POV camerawork. Other examples that are rich for analysis are documentary voiceovers and the narrative function they serve in 'anchoring' the meaning of the text.

Narrative is often seen as a universal category – we tell stories about what we did at the weekend and we apply editing principles. It is argued that most 'high concept' films are reworkings of seven classic Western stories that we use to understand our existence in limiting ways. Understood in this way, we can say that the principles of narrative sequencing are transferable to any media form. But there is a flexibility in form and structure, as Branston and Stafford describe:

> Narrative theory suggests that stories, in whatever media and whatever culture, share certain features, but particular media and cultures are able or driven to 'tell' stories in different ways. These differences are partly due to the nature of different media and technologies ('re-mediation') as well as the different audiences who use and enjoy them.
>
> (Branston and Stafford 2010: 57)

So how does this work for videogames? On the one hand, the construction of some game stories is reliant on the player progressing through the programme by trial and error and by learning so we are presented with a fundamentally more interactive form of narrative, compared to a film, say. The equivalent might be watching the first 20 minutes of a film ten times before moving on. So is game narrative linear? On the other hand, the narrative is only realized through the play actions of the audience and every narrative is unique to the gameplay enacted by the user.

There is a debate over whether games are narratives that you play or games that have stories. In many ways it depends on the game. Some argue that even *Harry Potter* games, despite their dependency on the film/book story are not really narratives in the 'normal' sense, simply because the player interacts and effectively 'writes' the action. Those that wish to apply classic narrative theory (such as Propp or Todorov) to games do so because they believe that games have basic stories that are clearly linked to classic myths, fables and 'handed down' story themes. However close a game might seem to the film, and thus to narrative theory, the unique nature of 'game time' (Newman 2004) makes this problematic. Whereas the films of *Harry Potter* employ two time frames – the time it takes for the narrative to be shown (a few hours) and the story time (several years) – the game doesn't share this distinction so easily. On the one hand, it is experienced always in the immediate present tense, but on the other, it can be paused, saved and returned to indefinitely. While this is also true of books and DVD versions of films, the interactive nature of the 'staggered' use of the game is different. This, then, is a story, but it's the story of your progress, just as any sports game also has a story of sorts, trying to win the World Cup in *Fifa*, for example.

NARRATOLOGY/LUDOLOGY

A 'narratologist', then, will see games as extensions of other forms of media, as spatial stories. And although they will have an easier time with *Harry Potter* than with *Fifa*, due to the former being so closely related to an existing narrative from literature and film, they will also try to extend the concept of narrative to analyse the latter. But a 'ludologist' will see the simulation element of both games as fundamental. The rule systems and types of play in each game will be of more value in analysing them from this perspective. And it is probably fair to say that the ludologist will have an easier time with *Harry Potter* than the narratologist will with *Fifa*.

Burn and Parker (2003) see videogames as using a 'narrative **multimodality**' that functions through a combination of inter-active and non-interactive elements (the cut scenes and information to be read/heard). These are mutually dependent. Alongside this dynamic, they describe three interdependent modalities that game narratives establish – the naturalistic modality (how the bits we control blend with those we don't), the technological modality (how we come to control the game) and the sensory modality (the way we believe that we are in the game, our sense of 'flow'). Frasca offers this response to the game narrative dilemma:

> The storytelling model is not only an inaccurate one but also it limits our understanding of the medium and our ability to create even more compelling. games. Unlike traditional media, videogames are not just based on representation but on an alternative semiotical structure known as simulation. Even if simulations and narratives do share some common elements (characters, settings and events) their mechanics are essentially different.
>
> (Frasca, in Wolf and Perron 2003: 221–2)

'Narratologists' think that games share narrative principles with older forms of linear media. Ludologists argue that the game player is doing something fundamentally different to the film viewer or novel reader. She is playing, not just watching or reading, so our analysis must begin with this distinction. Moreover, she is control-ling the **flow** of game time, whereas a TV viewer, even with live pause technology, is constrained by pre-ordained editorial decisions. Dovey and Kennedy summarize the argument:

> Meaning generated by play is different to meaning generated by reading. To read is to create meaning cognitively in the encounter with the text. To play is to generate meaning, to express it through play. Play allows us to actively express meaning (to be part of your clan, to be a stealth assas-sin or princess rescuing plumber). By playing out these roles we are temporarily inhabiting an avatar that functions as part of the gameplay and offers consumers a point of entry in to the game world.
>
> (Dovey and Kennedy 2006: 102)

TIME AND SPACE

C. Bazalgette (2009) suggests a helpful way of distinguishing types of texts in the online age that resists old/new media boundaries and also takes a 'raincheck' on adding more and more kinds of 'literacies' to the equation (literacy, new literacy, media literacy, game literacy, digital literacy, multimodal literacy and so on). Bazalgette distinguishes between time-based (linear) and space-based (non-linear) texts and suggests that contemporary literacy requires the ability to read and write both. Lawton and Cortes attempt a 'taxonomy of web-based media' with five categories: web-based traditional media (an online newspaper); reference media (for searching and retrieving); social networking media; gaming; and interpersonal communication. While Bazalgette wants to stop the 'flight' to an ill-defined notion of 'new literacy', Lawton and Cortes want to ask critical questions about the ability of the 'old literacy' to work in the digital world:

In what respects to the principles of media literacy, grounded in the traditional mass media, apply to the new media and in what respects should they be modified or enriched? In what respects do the new media require different, maybe unique approaches to and skills of media literacy?

(Lawton and Cortes, 2010: 17)

Prensky (2010) is concerned with ways in which Media Studies tends to focus on *nouns*, rather than *verbs*, in such discussions. For Prensky, the nouns change (books, newspapers, videogames, virtual worlds) but the verbs are constant (reading, writing, creating, being critical). The verbs of Media Studies are the key concepts we have covered in this chapter. Is Prensky right, that these can hold firm? Or will we need some new verbs as well?

NEW CONCEPTS

The notion that there are important shifts in the nature of identity or subjectivity attendant on the advent of digital media is evident across the diverse conceptual frameworks of new media studies. There is little agreement over the precise nature of these shifts, their historical and technological location, and their epochal import, but each – in different ways – makes claims for the importance of these shifts in understanding everyday life in a digital technoculture.

(Lister 2009: 285–6)

Chapter 5 on 'Changing Media' will deal more fully with the degree to which the classic toolkit for Media Studies that this chapter has introduced can 'hold firm' in the era of online media exchange or even the 'era of the prosumer'. But this chapter must conclude with a consideration of emerging concepts that seek to deal with the more complex interplay between media and people – Media Studies 'after the media', perhaps.

Consider the example of a YouTube fan/homage/remix video, *GTA in the Suburbs*, a reworking of play sequences from *Grand Theft Auto IV* in the 'real world' of (presumably) the producers. This text *can* be analysed using the classic conceptual toolkit. It has a variety of sub-generic elements of its own as well as those from the game which are parodying a set of film conventions in turn. It has a narrative that is switched and spliced with gameplay as a narrative and this needs to be 'unpacked' in terms of how players oscillate between in-game mission narrative and 'free time' in the online domain (see Kendall and McDougall 2009). The text represents many things – the game's meanings are remixed but left largely in place in an atmosphere of homage rather than challenge – there are things to say about gender, ethnicity, youth, urban culture, crime, sexuality and of course the text represents gameplayers to each other, as the playback and comments and countless alternative versions of the same idea testify. And we can move from this to a discussion about ideology and in particular capitalism and its 'rags to riches' subplot, played out in the gangster genre, hip hop and *Grand Theft Auto* (see Barrett 2006). However, the moments where the text departs from conventional ways of reading media are the most interesting, so to this existing conceptual repertoire we need to add such elements as playback, frivolity, discourse and diegesis. **Playback** is about the status of the text as in circulation, its meaning never fixed because its audience is an intrinsic part of the text. **Frivolity** is what we find when we spend more time doing ethnographic work with media users (such as game players) to find out how they are really thinking about the ideological elements at work in an event such as *Grand Theft Auto* – rarely do they take a serious view of this, more often they are 'playing' with the meanings set up by the game. **Discourse** describes ways of writing, talking and thinking about culture that tend to become conventional and it would appear that there is an important 'remix discourse' developing on YouTube that might need a new academic approach to understand it – representation and audience might not capture it. And **diegesis**, a concept that is part of the classic inventory of the critical media student, needs to be more prominent – where does the textual world begin and end, or does it?

However, whether we need these new concepts depends on whether we consider new media technologies to be reconfiguring cultural practices significantly enough and, more importantly perhaps, whether we decide that these 'new media' are really a transformation of media as opposed to a reorientation of 'old media'. There are no 'right answers' to this yet, but Chapter 5 on Changing Media engages with these debates in more detail.

SUMMARY

This chapter has introduced you to approaches to close reading of the 'micro' elements of media texts and ways of connecting them to 'macro' theoretical areas. The chapter started with the more straightforward textual analysis of still and moving images, using semiotics and looking at the ways in which meaning is conveyed through creative choices made with regard to camera, editing, sound and *mise èn scene*. Next, key concepts – genre, representation and narrative were introduced, and finally the more complicated debates regarding the status of such concepts in the wake of new digital media were set up.

The ideas and examples covered in this chapter can lead to the following summative statements:

* Semiotics is a tool for deconstructing the making of meaning at the level of the sign in a system of symbol and myth.
* Editing is hugely important in the construction of media meaning.
* Media texts can be analysed within intertextual networks of genre and convention.
* The same text can be looked at from different theoretical perspectives (for example, a film as the product of an auteur, a star or genre).

* Literacy, media literacy and the key concepts for Media Studies
  are challenged by new digital media and there are different
  views on the extent to which they can 'hold firm' and the need
  for new concepts.

FURTHER READING

All of the work referred to in this chapter is listed in the bibliography
at the end of the book, but the key recommended reading on the
material covered in this chapter is as follows:

KEY THEORIES

Genre theory: Altman (1999) is recommended.

Narrative theory: The formalists – Propp and Todorov – are
often used as a 'way in' to looking at narrative construction, as
well as Bordwell and Thompson for film, and more recently
the narratology/ludology debate for gaming – see Frasca for a
commentary on this and Carr for applications to games.

Theories of representation: Hall and the Birmingham School of
Contemporary Cultural Studies are usually the starting point,
then we move on to variations on the theme from the
likes of Mulvey, Barthes and Butler. Then Gauntlett's 'Media
Studies 2.0' idea suggest that the concept formally known as the
audience are now representing themselves.

Theories about audience: Students should engage with the work
of Ruddock, Hills, Barker, Buckingham and Hermes. All of
these writers challenge the old-fashioned idea that 'the audience'
can be easily pinned down to a particular 'reading' of a text, so
this area of Media Studies is now hotly contested.

Ideology: The 'classic' theories from Marx and Althusser are
applied to media by such writers as Winship and McRobbie and
more recently Jenkins ('Convergence Culture'). And contrasting
the political philosophies of Plato and Mill works well for con-
textualising the role of 'the media' in society in broader intellectual
debates about people and power.

Theories about culture: The field of Cultural Studies provides a
toolkit which is exemplified in the work of Miller, Hills,
Gauntlett and Jenkins with a view on how the 'classic' theories

of culture might work in the age of Web 2.0. Bennett, Kendall and McDougall go as far as to argue that Media Studies should move away from 'the media' as an object of study.

Theories about change: This is hard to pin down because of the delay in between writing a book like this and the publication date – and there's a chapter devoted to this later, but if the book was printed tomorrow, some key writers would be Anderson, Shirky, Jenkins (again), Fuller, Prensky, Leadbetter and, again, Gauntlett.

Theories about literacy: Gee and Bazalgette have made helpful contributions to debates around 'new literacies' and for a theoretical discussion of 'media literacy', Tyner, Buckingham, Marsh and Kendall are key agents.

KEY TEXTS

Altman, R. (1999) *Film/Genre*. London: BFI.
A classic theory of genre.

Bazalgette, C. (2009) 'Literacy in time and space', in *Points of View* 1. London: Media Education Association.
Offers a convincing new model for literacy and textual analysis.

Jenkins, H. (2006) *Convergence Culture: Where Old and New Media Collide*. New York: New York University Press.
Provides a framework for new modes of textual analysis to take account of convergence.

Lacey, N. (2010) *Image and Representation* 2nd edition. London: Macmillan.
Introduction to a long standing key concept for textual analysis.

Laughey, D. (2007) *Key Themes in Media Theory*. Maidenhead: Open University Press.
Covers the full range of theoretical schools of thought that inform textual analysis.

3

POWERFUL MEDIA
PEOPLE, POLITICS AND DEMOCRACY

AIMS

This chapter will introduce you to:

* the role of media in a democracy;
* theoretical ways of understanding and critically analysing the different ways in which media are used to exercise power;
* the power of media ownership;
* the power of media regulation;
* the complicated relationship between politics and media.

You are reading this book at the time of a major 'crossroads' for mass media. The key critical areas outlined in the five points above are under more scrutiny, and subject to more change, than perhaps at any time in the history of Media Studies. This means you are studying media in a very 'rich' time period for analysis. In the UK, in 2011, allegations of high-level collusion and corruption between tabloid newspapers, politicians and the police came to public attention. It became apparent that there was widespread use of phone hacking by tabloid journalists, often seriously unethical and illegal. The most serious evidence showed that the *News of the World* had been involved in hacking into the voicemail of a murdered schoolgirl, at the time she was missing, and even deleting messages to make room for any new ones. Worse still, there were allegations that senior executives in the huge multinational News Corporation, politicians and the police were complicit – or at least aware and failed to respond. We will cover the *News of the World* scandal (and subsequent closure) in detail shortly but to begin with we need to engage with their significance for 'macro' areas of Media Studies. When the production of news becomes the news, we can say, perhaps, as Anne Guest has it, that 'media will eat itself'. At the very least, it is not just conspiracy theorists who now believe in a *symbiotic relationship* between media, politicians and even the police. Furthermore, critical students of media in democracies such as the UK and the US now have to question their assumptions that they are looking at a 'free media' as opposed to 'undemocratic', state-controlled media. Where Marxist media theory might have looked outdated in the age of the prosumer, advanced capitalist economics and postmodern ways of looking at meaning and identity, the phone-hacking scandal that hit Rupert Murdoch's News Corporation, a plethora of high level UK politicians and the police force, lends considerable weight to this argument from R. Murray (2011):

> This is what a ruling class looks like – politicians who don't represent us, a media which doesn't inform us and police who don't protect us. The collapse of the once-imposing power of the Murdoch empire, a cornerstone of the network of class power in Britain for 30 years or more, has shone an unforgiving light of the larger workings of the set-up that controls the country.
>
> (R. Murray 2011: 12)

At no time in the recent lifespan of Media Studies has a statement from *The Morning Star* (the newspaper of the Communist Party) been so convincing. The role of a critical student of media, will be to weigh up such an argument in the face of evidence, and to consider alternative opinions. The key word is representation – of the public interest, of the people, of a plural society, and in a democracy, the question is always, how democratic is the media? Do we get the media we need, or the one we deserve? In order to answer such questions in the context of 'Hackgate', we need to go back to these more fundamental debates about media and power.

Figure 3.1 'Manufacturing consent' against the strike

Look at the image above. It was taken during a walk along the promenade in Scarborough on 16 June 2011, in the week that teachers and other public sector unions in the UK had voted in favour of industrial action.

There is widespread agreement that the 'power' of newspapers is declining, as more people turn to 24-hour/online news and less people spend money on newspapers. Rupert Murdoch and other newspaper owners are busy trying to harness the opportunities that the iPad and similar portable devices offer for a reformatted version of the traditional newspaper that is fit for this purpose, but there is a big question over whether this idea of the 'paywall' will work – the public have been 'groomed' for free news, it appears.

That aside, the everyday influence of media on our understanding of social life is an important part of Media Studies. You don't need to buy the *Scarborough Evening News* to read the bold headline in the picture – the same poster appeared all over the town on that day. And the headline is not a neutral account of events. The town is 'braced' for strike action, as it might be for a severe weather occurrence. The town will be passive in the wake of the action, the action will impact on the town. The town, as a collective term to describe its population, would not appear to include the teachers and other public sector workers who are taking this action. The complexity of the political, economic and industrial situation is reduced to 'strike action' versus 'the town'. Clearly the effects on the town will be bad and serious. Had the billboard stated 'workers forced to strike by government action' or 'striking workers braced for pension cuts', the representation of the events to come would be entirely different.

Now, there is no suggestion here that the passer-by on Scarborough promenade will be 'brainwashed' by this. Indeed any reception of media representations is negotiated and the reader's own socio-political interpretation is a major factor. But it's a good example to start with of what we mean by 'powerful media' – media images and messages carry values, they are loaded and the critical media student has the theoretical toolkit to deconstruct them.

There are so many aspects of the relationship between media and power in society that it is important to distinguish between some key critical questions that can't all be dealt with together.

* Do the people in power own the media and use it to influence us?
* Are the people who own media either under the influence of or working in partnership with other powerful people to support one another?

* What use of media do politicians make and in what ways might they need the media to be 'on message' with their policies?
* How important is 'media image' for politicians these days? Some say it is the most important thing in an election campaign, and that this has led to the rise of 'media spin' – never more scrutinized than at the time of writing this book, when public discussion was dominated by the *News of the World* phone-hacking scandal and revelations regarding high-level political influence.

Then there are questions about **regulation** – who has the power to decide what media we can and cannot have access to? What kinds of regulation are there, or should there be, to restrict media ownership so that some very rich and powerful businesses cannot simply 'buy up' more and more media companies? And if they do this, do they just acquire more and more economic power or do they also gain the means to influence the public? Also, there are more obvious and visible forms of media power (the reporting of events in a war, or a 'smear campaign' against a public figure or an allegation of 'media bias' or the control of film distribution by Hollywood companies in the UK).

Alongside these there are lots of examples of less clear and measurable forms of influence – the commercialization of childhood through media advertising, gender inequality through the cultivation of images of women as sexual objects in the media over decades. Or the power of the media to exclude people from minority groups – whether these be ethnically, culturally or sexually defined, or to do with age or disability – from mainstream media representations. Put simply, if the media rarely portray gay people as 'action heroes' but often portray them as 'camp' light entertainers, then the 'Cultivation theory' suggests that the media audience will come to stereotype gay people in that way, regardless of evidence in the real world. Of course, it gets more complicated when you consider the question of whether media stereotyping constructs or just represents our ideas, and whether people in particular groups end up reinforcing stereotypes themselves – 'acting the part'. As always with the study of media, it's complicated.

THE MATRIX

What is power, and who is in 'control'? These questions are foundations to a study of media power, but it isn't straightforward. It is better to think of power as a 'matrix' or a network or even an ecosystem, but to accept that any of these systematic approaches will have to be flexible because power is always in flux, always changing, never stable. According to Whittam-Smith (2011), the media and the financial markets are the two 'big powers' that can take on governments and win – so, thought about in this way, media have power in themselves and are not simply 'transmitters' of external power. Whittam-Smith cites the continuing power of the press, surfacing again in the UK in the form of the Ryan Giggs 'superinjunction' case and the rise of unregulated digital media as evidence of this power. He traces the development of this state of 'above regulation' media in the UK to the dominance (at least until 2011) of Rupert Murdoch, so we will consider both Giggs and Murdoch as important case studies with which to consider this statement:

> Where the power of the media is most objectionable is in their ability to deter governments from protecting us from their worst excesses.
>
> (Whittam-Smith 2011: 5)

CASE STUDY: RYAN GIGGS

In May 2011, in the UK Parliament, a Liberal Democrat MP named Ryan Giggs as the footballer who had taken out a 'superinjunction' to prevent details of his extra-marital affair being reported in the media. Although this action (available only to the affluent) worked, 75,000 people 'leaked' the information on Twitter. This had the unusual effect of creating a situation whereby the only people not able to comment on this were the 'mistress' and the mainstream media. The MP used 'Parliamentary privilege' to name Giggs and that paved the way for newspapers to follow up the story. Parliamentary privilege protects Members of Parliament from the law so they can speak freely on public matters during debates, without fear of being sued for libel, slander, defamation or of being prosecuted under the Official Secrets Act. Compared to the use of Twitter in the

'Arab Spring', this is a trivial issue. But in terms of its impact on media regulation and law, it was very 'heavyweight', and thus of huge importance for the study of contemporary media, as is made clear by this statement from David Cameron, the UK Prime Minister:

It's not fair on the newspapers if all the social media can report this and the newspapers can't and so the law and the practice have got to catch up with how people consume media today. I don't think there's an easy answer to this.

(in the *Guardian*, 24 May 2011)

This theme – of having to 'catch up' with changes in technology and modes of media exchange – is one we keep returning to. Crucially, these events hinge on the vexed issue of 'public interest', set against privacy. It is almost impossible to protect the privacy of celebrities without endangering serious investigative journalism, which is at the cornerstone of any democratic media. It seems we can't have one without the other. Furthermore, if the rich and powerful are able to protect themselves from being reported on by purchasing the silence of journalists in this way, then what are the implications for democracy?

POWERFUL MEDIA: MICRO AND MACRO

Broadly speaking, the theoretical ideas and approaches covered in this chapter will be concerned with 'political economy' and 'ideology', which are often connected but start out from different academic positions. Political economy (macro) is more concerned with a factual, institutional understanding of how media are produced and circulated. This will include ownership, finance, politics, regulation and law. Analysis of **ideology** is far more textual (micro) – decoding and deconstructing messages at work in media texts and how these are patterned and structured across texts. For our purposes in introducing the key concepts required to study media, we can view these as interrelated, there is a dynamic and powerful relationship, then, between the ownership of media production and distribution and the dominant ideas that are reinforced in media texts. This is a changing landscape, especially in the context of new social media but academics tend to agree on the ongoing importance of the political economy approach, however great the changes in the context of mediation.

Everything we consider in this chapter hinges on ideas about what kind of media we ought to have in a democracy, but this is more complicated than it might appear at first glance, since democracy in action is far from straightforward. So, first, it's essential to have a firm grasp of what democracy means in practice.

DEMOCRACY

There is a good deal of muddle about democracy ... the muddle of democracy is due to a genuine confusion as to what democracy is supposed to be about.

(MacPherson 1966: 1)

I am happy to confess that the visions I had as a youth for peace, justice and democracy worldwide have become more important to me now that I have had eighty-five plus years of experience and I cannot be dismissed on the grounds that when I grow up I will see things differently.

(Benn 2010: 147)

Tony Benn urges his grandchildren, and future generations, to pose five questions to anyone in power:

What power have you got?
How did you get it?
In whose interests do you exercise it?
To whom are you accountable?
How do we get rid of you?

To see how this works in daily life, consider those five questions in relation to: a) any unelected dictator (at the time of writing, Colonel Gaddafi in Libya was a good example); b) any elected politician who represents you where you live; c) one of your teachers or employers; d) Rupert Murdoch; and d) Simon Cowell, the super-rich creator of *The X Factor*.

A grasp of the process of democracy is an essential starting point. Democracy relates to power, control, citizenship and freedom.

Comparing two very different political philosophers such as Plato and John Stuart Mill is a useful way in to this.

THE REPUBLIC

Plato (whose ideas were 'written up' by Socrates in 420 BC, see Plato 1987) asserted that there are different categories of human beings and there is little point in letting the second and third classes of citizens believe they are socially mobile in any way. A society functions, and people are actually happier, if they 'know their place' and stay in it. The ruling elite make decisions, the middle class 'guardians' make it all happen and inform the lower orders (the workers, who are essentially slaves) about what is to be done. The only use for art, in Plato's doctrine, was to distract the workers from reality, to keep them entertained in blissful ignorance of how society is being organized and how, looked at another way, they are being exploited by those in power. Many recent and contemporary media texts explore this idea – the *Matrix* film trilogy and *The Truman Show* are modern-day reworkings of Plato's simile of the cave and work on the same principle – is it better to know the painful truth or to stay in a fictional reality? The Marxist view of this is that it constructs a 'false consciousness' and the challenge is for the working classes to resist such ideologies and discover the truth about their exploitation but the Platonic view would be to argue that they won't be any happier and society will cease to function if everyone has 'ideas above their station'. Before we complacently assume that Plato was a fascist and his ideas are not applicable to our times, consider the educational system, in which the rich and privileged generally access the more 'prestigious' schools and universities and, in the UK, the continued interest in the monarchy – even during the harshest economic period in living memory, thousands turned out on the streets of London to celebrate the marriage of a prince – might this, and the ongoing obsession with 'talent TV' (such as *The X Factor*) be part of the kind of 'distraction' Plato was advocating?

So Plato's idea of a functioning society (his 'Republic') depends on a denial of freedom – people are to be ruled, kept in place and distracted from any questioning of how the system is constructed.

LIBERTY

A very different, liberal, political philosophy is demonstrated in the work of John Stuart Mill, who was writing in a very different time period (the 19th century) but offers a useful contrast to Plato. For Mill's idea of 'utilitarian liberty' (see Mill 1986) the principle is that any society should function on the maxim of providing the highest possible amount of freedom for citizens, who can determine their own actions entirely up to the point where their actions can be seen to harm others. People, then, are never to be 'kept in their place' but instead can be self-fulfilling as long as they adhere to this 'self-regarding' principle. But it's never very easy to pin down the point at which an action stops being self-regarding and starts being other-regarding. Consider these examples:

* Breaking wind;
* Smoking;
* Gambling;
* Paying for a sex-worker to assault you in the privacy of your own home.

The first example is generally taken to be a socially embarrassing but fairly trivial, even amusing case. The second is, in some countries, now the subject of state intervention, the response to the third is culturally-specific and, unlike smoking, which is now seen by many as always harmful to others, gambling is often discussed in terms of the extent to which it impacts on the economic circumstances of others (for example, debt). The most difficult one is the fourth. At first glance, many say 'the only person suffering here is the person being assaulted' (although, presumably, if one pays for the action, then the 'suffering' would be a form of pleasure). However, if we think through the issues at length, we might consider the way that a system of exploitation – sex workers being forced into the industry, the relationship between the sex industry, addiction, trafficking and exploitation of various kinds – is being supported by this action. So we end up needing to analyse the relationship between the private sphere (our individual actions) and its impact on the public sphere (the lives of others). It is, then, very complicated.

A **democratic** society is one in which elected and accountable human beings are given the power to make decisions about the kinds of things we have outlined here on behalf of, and impacting on, the rest of us. If we don't like the decisions, we have a chance to replace the people making them with others – so they are accountable to us. This is at the heart of Tony Benn's five questions. In any society that is not anarchistic, people will have power over other people. But that becomes dangerous only in the absence of accountability. For MacPherson (1966), whose statement about the 'muddle' of democracy we began with, the liberal-democratic state (one of which you are quite likely to be living in if you are studying media) is defined by welfare and regulation. The government provides health and education to all, but regulates us more than would be the case if we were left to survive without those things. Where media fit into this is very interesting – how free can media providers be from the state, who controls the flow of information and in whose interests? In a purely capitalist system, media is like any other industry and media providers can do whatever they want to make money. In a communist regime (such as China or Cuba) or an unelected dictatorship of another kind, media will be explicitly controlled by the state and used to convey their information and view of the world to the masses. In a liberal democracy, the state and media providers have a more complex and uneasy relationship, one that is tested out on a daily basis by contests over ownership, freedom of information and privacy laws.

Such a detailed context is crucial because, as we said at the start of the chapter, analysing the relationship between power, media and democracy is only possible if we have a clear sense of what democracy is – how democratic our media can be is a question that can only be answered with this political–philosophical understanding secure.

DEWEY'S YARDSTICK

In the American context, the ideas of John Dewey have long been influential in helping people understand how education, community and public sphere information (in our times, media) do more or less to construct a sense of citizenship in a society at a given time. The extent to which media, and other public sphere agents of influence (schools, for example) appear to be open and accessible for people to have a voice or appear to be most concerned with excluding access and distracting people from decision-making (through excessive examining in education or an abundance of trivial entertainment in media, perhaps) will shape the nature of democratic practice:

> Dewey believed that the emergence of a modern mass media had the potential to improve the conditions and operations of American democracy, if structured with those ends in mind, but he worried that the particular shape of the American media system, governed primarily by commercial interests, would have a much more negative influence.
>
> (Press and Williams 2010: 75)

So Dewey provided a kind of 'yardstick' for media students to use when looking at the extent to which media in a society at any given time is democratic. What is the balance between public interest and commercial interest? And what is the relationship between the accessibility of the media and the accessibility of the public sphere more broadly? Of course, these questions are complicated yet further by the impact of the Internet as the idea of measuring the democratic nature of a single nation's media is much harder when citizens are globally connected.

CASE STUDY: NEWS AGENDAS

An interesting way in to a consideration of how news agendas operate to **gatekeep** the flow of information in a society is *Wag the Dog*, a film from 1997, directed by Barry Levinson and starring Dustin Hoffman and Robert De Niro. In this film, a discredited president, facing election defeat, is persuaded by a 'spin doctor' to construct a fake war to be reported through US television with a famous Hollywood director hired to construct the media operation. The task is very simple, watch the film and answer this question: *could it be done?* Here is a response to that question from media student Kerri Harris (Newman University College, Birmingham, UK, 2010):

> In the film, the main 'team' responsible for controlling the distribution of information for the president, and his public

image all state that none of them voted for him during the last election. To me, this meant that it didn't matter who won the election, who became president, they would be doing the same job no matter what, the president is just their puppet. A face for the voting public.

The news service is definitely not democratic, the news was controlled and organized, the viewing public only got to see what the people in power wanted them to see. I would say this was almost a cross between Authoritarian and Soviet media (using the classic models of media systems, Siebert et al. 1963).

I don't think that constructing a fantasy war would be able to happen today, the world is shrinking, communication between countries and people is much more advanced. Social networking sites mean the distribution of information is readily available, even if countries try and stop it (China, Iraq) the tweets still get through.

We can unpack various threads in this response that will help to frame an approach to studying news agendas in the context of media and power. First, Harris identifies a cynical idea at the heart of the film about the extent to which political leaders are really in charge of anything, if the film reflects reality, it means the 'mediation' of politics is at such an advanced stage that the people who appear to be in power are really little more than actors – 'a face for the voting public' – this would be an indictment of democracy. Secondly, Harris relates the news service depicted in the film to real 'authoritarian' news models she has studied, these are state-controlled, profoundly undemocratic media systems, so it would be ironic for the US ('home of the free') to be operating in a similar way. Most importantly, though, Harris locates the implausibility of the plot not in the intent (she doesn't say that no government would think of doing such a thing) but instead in the way that social media would make it very difficult, citing China and Iraq as places where she has observed 'the people' resisting official media strategy by using the affordances and connections of the Internet – 'the tweets still get through'.

MODELS OF NEWS PRODUCTION

It is very important, but equally very difficult, for a media student to develop an international understanding of media power, and one fairly straightforward comparison you can make is to look at how news is produced in a range of countries. The key distinctions will relate to ownership, political structure, regulation and journalistic practices/codes of conduct. Realizing that media production is not the same from country to country allows us to engage more critically with our own news provision. This is particularly important for students in the UK or US – who have, relatively speaking, similar media structures and may be forgiven for mistaking these to be universal. Oates (2008) provides a comparative analysis which defines the US system as 'libertarian' (very little publicly-funded news media); the UK system as split (with broadcast news regulated for social responsibility and the free press operating in the US-style libertarian model) and the Russian news media as state-regulated (despite appearances that the 'Neo-Soviet' system is not so). Oates traces the distinctions by using a model with key elements – political environment, media norms, regulation, ownership and journalistic practices. So the production of news is the outcome of these four determinants:

Examining these elements of the News Production Model reveals a range of constraints that will shape news content. These constraints start long before a journalist arrives at his or her desk in the morning to begin the task of covering events and gathering news. All of these elements will dictate the shape, direction, and final form of news coverage. That, in turn, will influence the citizens and the public sphere.

(Oates 2008)

In a democracy, the public have an entitlement to a 'free press'. This is a liberal idea and the extent to which it is realistic in a capitalist world is the question that underpins most of what we are dealing with in this chapter. This key question of whether this freedom can be protected in a society where the rich and powerful have interests that are at odds with the liberal ideal is taken up by Marxist analyses of media:

Liberal theory argues that the press – and mass media in general – serve democracy in three ways. They play a key role in informing the electorate. They provide a means of overseeing and 'checking' in government – the watchdog role. They articulate public opinion ... a Marxist perspective holds that as mass media organisations are owned and operated by ruling, or elite groups in society, the individuals running them will ensure that these institutions reinforce the dominant ideology in a way that appears to be 'common sense', thus helping maintain class inequalities.

(D. Barlow and Mills 2009: 41)

One such individual is Rupert Murdoch.

RUPERT MURDOCH

The Australian 'tycoon' Rupert Murdoch started owning media institutions in the early 1950s and since then he has come to acquire for his News Corporation a vast array of newspapers, TV channels, radio stations, film companies and websites. In the UK he owns a large amount of BSkyB – and was set to increase that share in order to merge the companies, thus acquiring a much greater level of control over media in Britain. However, this bid was withdrawn in 2011 as a result of the phone-hacking scandal that caused him to close the *News of the World*.

In July 2011, News Corporation owned a significant share in ITV and BSkyB as well as The *Sun* and *The Times*. In the US, Murdoch owns the Fox Broadcasting Company, 20th Century Fox, *The New York Post*, Dow Jones, HarperCollins, National Geographic and a range of pay TV channels. As well as MySpace, the multinational also owns significant media activity in Germany, Italy, Australia, China and broader South East Asia and India. The dividends amount to about $30 billion (McMahon et al. 2011). This is what is known as a 'media empire' and, with its global reach, News Corporation has always been the subject of much concern, with people thinking that the deregulation of media ownership in the UK, started by Margaret Thatcher when she was Prime Minister and continued by Tony Blair and Gordon Brown under New Labour, has allowed him to become so powerful that he now has influence over the way political events in particular are reported. When the phone-hacking scandal came to public attention, UK politicians clamoured to condemn Murdoch when months before (and for years preceding) they had allowed a 'cosy relationship' to work in Murdoch's favour – a benign influence over UK politics.

The 2004 documentary film *Outfoxed,* directed by Robert Greenwald, is an important film for anyone concerned with Murdoch's relationship with his journalists – the commercial and political agenda in relation to the editorial agenda. One particular sequence stands out as a challenge to the idea of news/current affairs broadcasting as a neutral 'window on the world'. It features the appearance on the Fox network's *Bill O'Reilly Show* of the son of a port authority worker killed on 9/11 who refused to sanction the 'war on terror'. The guest is told to 'shut up' by O'Reilly, escorted from the studio and later becomes the victim of a sustained campaign to discredit his views about the Bush administration's response to the attacks on New York. The key issue is about audience and distribution. If we agree (as the makers of *Outfoxed* certainly want us to) that Fox News is anything but impartial, then the fact that Fox is a global network, thanks to satellite and digital access, may have serious international implications. The concern is that Murdoch's 'neoconservative' perspective on news events comes to determine what is seen as newsworthy, what gets reported, how it gets reported and how the aftermath of news events get discussed. Crucially, this view suggests that a neoconservative ideology comes to be seen as 'the norm' across the globe – a politically biased perspective masquerading as impartial.

Murdoch (and his son James, the 'heir to the throne') already had a major challenge in this century to preserve the economic value of news in the wake of social media but this ongoing struggle paled spectacularly into the shadows in comparison to the phone-hacking scandal of June 2011.

In 2011, Murdoch was poised to secure a majority share in BSkyB – subject to approval by the UK government. The lead-up to this decision was already the subject of much political and cultural debate when, in July 2011, one of the biggest media scandals of all-time hit the headlines – the revelation of widespread illegal phone-hacking by journalists at one of Murdoch's most successful tabloid news-papers and, even more damaging allegations that a former editor, subsequently employed by the UK Prime Minister as press secretary, and senior executives at News International were complicit in covering this up. If this were not already serious enough, allegations followed that the phone of a murdered teenager (missing at the time of the incident) and a mother of a child abuse victim with whom the paper had been campaigning for a change to the law had both been hacked by a private investigator employed by the newspaper. In the case of the missing teenager, this had allegedly given her parents false hope that she might still be alive and in the case of the campaigning mother, when the paper closed this was held up as a beacon of investigative good practice, so the claim that all the while the paper had been hacking the phone of the woman they were campaigning with was seen as morally bankrupt. Add to the mix the allegation that police officers had been paid for information and this created a 'perfect storm' that led to Murdoch first closing the paper, making Sunday 10 July 2011 its final edition and then retrieving his bid for more shares of BSkyB.

FLAT EARTH NEWS

Davies (2009) painted a damning picture of journalistic practices that seemed to be alarmingly borne out by the phone-hacking scandal of 2011. In *Flat Earth News*, he exposes a vast number of 'deals' between journalists and politicians and a broad set of examples of the news being explicitly controlled to serve the interests of the powerful. Equally disturbing is the openly discriminatory nature of contemporary newsrooms:

> Perhaps I have been unlucky, but I have never come across a reporter from the *Daily Mail* who did not have a similar story, of black people being excluded from the paper because of their colour. A district reporter told me he would call up from Manchester to tell the news desk a story, and they would always ask: 'Are they our kind of people?' i.e. Are they white, middle class? Or more often it would be: 'Are they of the dusky hue?' And if they were of the dusky hue, they didn't want the story.
>
> (Davies 2009: 371)

CASE STUDY: THE *NEWS OF THE WORLD*

On 10 July 2011, the *News of the World* published its final edition. The paper had been running since 1843 but in early July 2011, on a daily basis, more and more revelations about illegal and deeply unethical phone-hacking and allegations regarding corrupt payments to police officers led to Murdoch closing down the paper with commentators viewing this as an attempt to limit the damage to News Corporation as a whole. In the aftermath of the closure, the UK public began to question deeply for the first time since the 1980s, what Henry Porter described as Murdoch's 'perversion of politics by and for Rupert Murdoch'. Campaigning journalist John Pilger had for decades been exposing what he called 'The Murdoch Effect' on the UK press, but the hegemonic discourse had managed to marginalize this view as being outdated in the era of market forces and 'the information society'. Now, Porter and others were returning to the serious question of how the political elite had allowed this situation to develop to this extent and Murdoch's attempt to take over a majority share in BSkyB to merge it with News Corporation came under a much higher level of public scrutiny. Porter viewed this as a key turning point in the nature of UK political media:

> The king is dead – long live democracy. With the immolation of the *News of the World*, we saw the end of the pre-eminent political influence of the last three decades in Britain. Rupert Murdoch's pass to Number 10 has been withdrawn, the access code for his editors and senior executives has expired. All the unseen deal-making, fixing, manipulation and bullying has gone.
>
> (Porter 2011: 36)

BBC journalist Paul Mason makes a broader argument in response to the crisis at the heart of the 'Murdoch empire' and the exposure of its unethical relationship with UK politicians, suggesting that these events provide a contemporary endorsement of Chomsky's 'Manufacturing Consent' thesis and also the 'conspiracy theory' logic of *The Wire*, in which politicians, media and business are all connected in 'the game':

> It is like a nightmare scripted by Noam Chomsky and Slavoj Zizek: key parts of the political machinery of Britain are wavering.
>
> (Mason 2011: 1)

But Mason also observes that social media's crucial role in events serves to outdate the Chomsky model. Consent can be more easily dismantled when, in this context:

> Large corporations pulled their advertising because the scale of the social media response allowed them to know what they are obsessed with knowing: the scale of the reputational threat to their own brands. Where all this leaves Noam Chomsky's theory I will rely on the inevitable wave of comments from its supporters to flesh out. But the most important fact is: not for the first time in 2011, the network has defeated the hierarchy.
>
> (Mason 2011: 1)

Natalie Fenton, looking at the problem from the more objective position of the media academic, perhaps (as opposed to the journalist's view) is more guarded in her assessment. Fenton argues that a new framework for defining 'public interest' is more important than closing down newspapers and public enquiries into corruption. According to Fenton, the corporate, deregulated 'market forces' news model has caused a crisis in the relationship between news and democracy in the digital age, as journalists' obligation to 'self-regulate' is in conflict with the need to publish quickly and to the largest possible degree of interest, a trend she describes as 'faster and shallower corporate journalism'.

> The phone hacking saga shows that a marketised and corporatised media cannot be relied upon to deliver the conditions for deliberative democracy to flourish. Markets do not have democratic intent at their core. When markets fail or come under threat or simply become too bullish, ethical journalistic practice is swept aside in pursuit of competitive gain and financial stability.
>
> (Fenton 2011: 1)

The final, and crucial point to note about these events is this. When the decision is made by the UK state about whether Murdoch can be allowed, in the wake of these revelations, to acquire a larger share in the UK media the criteria employed will be the degree to which the plurality of media is undermined:

> For a number of years, I've felt that the debate around 'media plurality' has remarkable echoes of that surrounding climate change. Both concern our capacity to find a sustainable balance within a complex and delicate ecosystem, one in which the true scale of the problem only becomes apparent when you sift through the evidence and consider the frightening ramifications of getting it wrong.
>
> (Puttnam 2011: 37)

When plurality is weakened, a state of hegemony pervades. This is a Marxist idea, and the News International scandal in 2011 provides, for the critical media student, a rich connection to such 'classic' theories of power and ideology.

MARXIST THEORIES OF POWER

A central Marxist theory that is often used in relation to media power is 'hegemony':

> A state of hegemony is achieved when a provisional alliance of certain social groups exerts a consensus that makes the power of the dominant group appear both natural and legitimate. Institutions such as the mass media, the family, the education system and religion, play a key role in the shaping of people's awareness and consciousness and thus can be agents through which hegemony is constructed, exercised and maintained.
>
> (Watson and Hill 2003: 126)

There is distinction between Marx and Marxism which is rather obvious but nonetheless important. Marx's theories are his own work and Marxist theory is the adaptation and development of his thinking which is still happening today – so we have 'New Marxism', 'Marxist feminism' and other variations. Marx himself did not write about 'the media' as such, but his theories – particularly around *ideology* – have been applied to media for generations, and will continue to be applied into the future, for sure.

Three Marxist theorists are particularly useful in the study of media power. The first is Karl Marx himself who famously declared (see Elster 1986) that the people who rule in any society do so not only by controlling the means of production (the ways of making money – in his day this would be land and factories but in our times we can think about Rupert Murdoch, Richard Branson and Bill Gates who own, and are striving to keep control of, the means by which information is exchanged) but also the production of ideas. In other words they keep the rest of us in place by making sure that we share their ideas about 'the way things should be'. The British monarchy still proves this. If we wanted to, we could throw the Royal family out of their homes and demand that we no longer fund their lives through our taxes but we don't because of a consensus shared by many that this elitist hierarchy is understood as 'heritage' and 'tradition'. The amazing level of interest in the 2011 Royal Wedding is evidence of this – it took place at a time of sweeping cuts and job losses, and yet the nation was seemingly transfixed by this marriage, convened by a super-rich family, largely at the public's expense (the singer Morrissey controversially labelled the Royal Family 'benefit scroungers' in the lead-up to the spectacle).

The Marxist thesis is that we don't do very much about the unfair nature of the capitalist system because we are convinced that everyone has the chance to become Alan Sugar, or a similar 'rags to riches' role model (which is clearly not the case as the system cannot allow everyone to succeed) and because we cannot think of a viable alternative.

Althusser (in Easthope and McGowan 2004) was a Marxist who developed this idea by distinguishing between two forms of state control – Repressive State Apparatuses (RSAs), these are physical, 'concrete' ways of controlling us, such as the law, the police, the army, and Ideological State Apparatuses (ISAs), the media, the Church, education. The point is simple – you don't need the RSAs if the ISAs work. People won't challenge the system if the ISAs are all working to make it seem natural and fair, so the ISAs, including the media, work to create consensus.

Gramsci was the Marxist intellectual who developed the idea of hegemony, which we started with, to explain the importance of this constructed consensus. In a famous book and subsequent documentary about the media's role in all of this, Noam Chomsky (2002) described how consent is 'manufactured'. This is a theory of media propaganda that sees the central function of media as being to serve the interests of the powerful who own, control and use media to convey and reinforce their values. In the Chomsky version of propaganda theory, media texts don't tell lies, or distort the truth but in general terms oppositional points of view or broader contexts for political events are filtered out – a process of '**gatekeeping**' which marginalizes dissent and reproduces **hegemonic** processes. A criticism of Chomsky is that, like Adorno, he reduces media audiences to a passive mass – in his words the 'bewildered herd' (Chomsky 2002: 21).

In simple terms, then, such theories aim to prove that we are manipulated by those in power – who control the media – to think we are agreeing with dominant ideas, which we come to think of as our own ideas. A much more recent example of the manufacturing of consent is explored by the 2004 *Outfoxed* documentary, which sought to expose the incredible levels of editorial control imposed by Rupert Murdoch on the journalistic practices at work in the US Fox News network and more recently by the idea that the *News of the World* crisis provides a contemporary endorsement of Chomsky's model.

The campaigning journalist John Pilger is another commentator engaged in a propaganda model approach to news reporting. Writing originally, along with Chomsky, about the American manufacturing of anti-Communist 'consent', Pilger has regularly updated his work to account for more recent events, such as the reporting of conflict in East Timor, Afghanistan and what he sees as bias in the representation of Palestine–Israel tension by the American news media. Pilger, as a journalist, does not seek to present an academic model, only to expose injustices in news reporting.

Neither Noam Chomsky or John Pilger would necessarily describe themselves bluntly as 'Marxist', but it is clear that their work is premised on the Marxist theory that those in power use the media to reinforce their own ideological positions so it is important to redress the balance by exposing this.

CULTURAL IMPERIALISM

More space will be devoted to this theory in Chapter 4 on Global Media. An element of broader 'postcolonial' theory, this approach views media as part of a contemporary empire building strategy. Living in an era where powerful nations no longer seek more power by, in general, reaching out across the world through military force, they manage this through the 'spread' of culture, which, 'Trojan horse' like, invades our ideologies. Media is only a part of this, it is important to state, working together with education, religion, customs and language. There is something of a 'chicken and egg' question here also. If we consider the dominance of Hollywood films in the UK, we could find the reasons in a political economy analysis that locates power in the vertical integration of cinema – the chains of multiplexes, modes of distribution and production are owned by the same American companies. Or we could locate it in a cultural imperialist model – British film-goers speak the same language as Americans and, as such, are influenced unwittingly by this constant diet of American ideology conveyed through film, to the extent that films produced in the UK and across Europe are rarely seen. In this way, American storytelling takes on a universal appearance when it is anything but. Or we could simply attribute the success of Hollywood films across the globe to their high production values and the marketing budgets allocated to them – the 'market forces' model will simply reveal the audience expressing its preference. Either way, the outcome**, cultural imperialism** theorists such as Schiller (1997) argue is a state of 'cultural homogenization' – the McDonald's effect ('McWorld' – the same American food on offer in every city) is replicated in culture and in media representations. Another complex element of this is the theoretical idea of 'the other', whereby the dominant media-producing groups construct representations of other nations or cultures as 'different' and this is cultivated over time on a global scale – again, a particular representation masquerades as 'the norm'. Said (1995) describes one example of this as 'orientalism' – people from the East are thus portrayed as 'other' to the (Western) norm. More recent concerns about media representations of Islam are influenced by Said's approach. Laughey makes sense of the relationships between these various related theories of cultural power as sharing a 'postcolonial' approach:

> Whereas colonialism refers to political and military occupation of another nation, postcolonialism can be understood as a more covert

form of occupation that does not require physical invasion but is
instead linked to processes of media and cultural imperialism.

(Laughey 2007: 142)

Said's work has many connections with the 'discourse theory' of
Foucault who argued that discourse (ways of representing the world
in language in terms that appear, but are never 'objective') is the
carrier of power. So the study of media is the study of discourse, and
thus the study of power. Critical discourse analysis is a framework for
locating and analysing how such power is 'exercised'.

CRITICAL DISCOURSE ANALYSIS

The most influential writer in this field is Fairclough (1995), who
provides a framework for analysing, at the micro level, political
media discourse. Here, then, we are dealing with the use *of* media
by politicians, or the political discourse *in* media texts. Fairclough
draws on some key theoretical ideas about discourse from Bourdieu
(1984) and Foucault (1980) and uses these to develop a more specific
account of intertextual media discourse. This is concerned with the
ways that individual texts are framed by, and received with reference
to, a broader range of other texts that create 'orders of discourse' –
ways of communicating that become 'the norm' in a particular
field – for example, news journalism. Using Fairclough's model to
analyse what he calls 'mediatized political discourse' (Fairclough
1995: 161), a media student will identify the key agents involved
in political media discourse (for example, politicians, journalists,
experts of various kinds, the ordinary public); genres of media texts
(such as political interviews, debate shows, magazine columns); and
the framing and reception of texts (how texts are inter-related and
how this sets up particular kinds of reading of them by audiences).
The difference with this more 'sociolinguistic', textual approach to
locating political power in media is that its focus is on the complexity of the discourse rather than on a broader, more basic idea
about media texts 'transmitting' ideologies, or in Fairclough's words,
'the link between texts and society/culture is seen as mediated by
discourse practices' (Fairclough 1995: 143).

Critical media students, then, need to map these broad, 'macro'
theories to 'micro' examples of contemporary media representation

where they can be understood as constructing or reinforcing 'othering' discourses about groups of people. These 'others' can be marginalized in this way on the basis of ethnicity, sexuality, regional identity, (dis)ability, age or any other socio-cultural 'marker' that sets them up as different to the 'norms' associated with the dominant social group in the culture. Ramone (2011) finds a contemporary example, which is particularly close to home (ironically, perhaps, in the 'globalizing' context that follows) for the author of this book, in a recent advert for Cadbury's Dairy Milk, in which 'the advert celebrates the 101-year trading relationship with Ghana by representing the country as a kind of African Willy Wonka's chocolate factory, a place of constant, joyful cocoa production. These images suggest simplicity, small-scale community farming and certainly not mass production' (Ramone 2011: 10). Ramone goes on to explain how the 'othering' of Ghana, intended as positive – all the 'organic' attributes that global chocolate production cannot claim to represent, reinforces colonial attitudes towards African coffee production, along with Fairtrade initiatives and charity work, both of which are constructed along 'missionary' lines which are well intentioned but framed by cultural intervention which reduces, by 'othering' the identity of the producers.

FEMINIST THEORIES OF POWER

Feminist media theory is a complex range of approaches and must never be reduced to simplistic definitions. However, a shared analytical pursuit is the questioning of powerful gender norms that are reinforced to a greater or lesser extent in media, and the relationship between media representations of gender and inequalities in broader social life:

> Historically people and movements have been called feminist when they recognised the connections between social inequalities, deprivations and oppressions and gender differences.
>
> (Humm 1992: 403)

It's a tall order to summarize a feminist approaches to the power exercised by media in a section of this size in an introductory text such as this, particularly when the author is male. But that said, we can construct the following basic overview. The key distinction to begin with is between femaleness as a biological/sexual category, 'femininity' as a socially/culturally constructed set of ideas about the female gender and **feminism** as a political position – the struggle for equality and/or the celebration of gender difference (these two are different sides of the political coin). If, reading this, you don't see a feminist politics as less straightforwardly important as anti-racism or anti-homophobia, then a feminist analysis of this would state that, in our contemporary 'enlightened' society, women are still marginalized in everyday discourse in so much as sexist jokes or comments and everyday misogyny are treated as 'just banter' in a way that racist statements would not be. The media, of course, play a big role in reinforcing these ideas – from the fact that both magazines for men and for women feature women on the cover, to be looked at by both genders, to the use by the current UK Prime Minister of the TV advert catchphrase 'calm down, dear' when disagreeing with a female MP in the House of Commons.

So there is a broad, shared commitment by all versions of feminist media analysis that media texts and media discourse undermine gender equality and reinforce patriarchal 'common sense'/ideology as 'the norm'. But different feminist approaches have contrasting ways of seeing/accounting for this kind of media power. Such contrasting approaches include Marxist feminism; black feminism; feminist psychoanalysis; Arab feminism; feminist cultural materialism, poststructuralist feminism (or French feminism) and post-feminism. Whereas a Marxist feminist position will account for broad patriarchal ideology in media, locating women as subordinate, rather than the working classes more generally and in this way seeing men as 'the ruling class' controlling the production of ideas in and through media; a poststructuralist position will identify, in textual practices, a set of binary oppositions with positive/negative values – head/heart, logos/pathos, father/mother and then look at how women are constructed in subtle ways as 'other' to the (male) norm. Laura Mulvey's (1975) highly influential theory of 'the male gaze' argues that, in cinema, the camera constructs an apparently 'objective' view of events through a male perspective. In this sense, the male is active (looking) and the female is passive (an object to be looked at). This, of course, can be extended to magazine covers. Winship (1987) argues that 'the gaze between cover model and women readers marks the complicity between women seeing themselves in the image which the masculine culture has defined'. This, in turn, resonates with the Marxist idea developed in Althusser's (1977) notion of 'interpellation' – the social/ideological practice of misrecognizing yourself. If we put these two together, a feminist–Marxist reading of magazine covers is straightforward – Winship's notion of *complicity* is about us being prepared, for the reward of gratification, to recognize the ideal version of ourselves, despite the anxiety this will cause (when we compare our real appearance to the ideal). For feminists, the male culture reinforces its power by defining women in this way and encouraging this anxiety. The Marxist term for this is '**false consciousness**'. Through a range of cultural reinforcements – a process of **cultivation** – of which magazines are just one, women are distracted from the inequality in our society. Instead of asking for equal pay and creating more positive representation in the media, women are commenting on the waistlines of celebrities.

The work of Judith Butler (1990) sets up gender as entirely cultural and an act of performance, suggesting 'gender trouble' – the deliberate subversion (or 'queering') of gendered behaviour as a political response:

> That the gendered body is performative suggests that it has no ontological status apart from the various acts which constitute its reality.
>
> (Butler 1990: 185)

Butler is saying here that it is only our collective daily performances of gender that make it what it is. It does not exist outside of these performances, so we are not performing anything that existed beforehand (this is 'ontology'). Subverting these kinds of performances, then, does not simply mean constructing clearly alternative versions of 'being male' or 'being female', but instead there is a premium on parody and pastiche and these elements sometimes connect a feminist media theory to **postmodernism**, which we shall turn to next. For this reason, Lady Gaga is discussed as a postmodern 'agent' of feminist pastiche.

LADY GAGA

According to Bacon et al. (2010), postmodern feminism challenges the notion of fixed gender categories. These categories carry power, in media discourse, so undermining them through subversion is an act of resistance to such power. Lady Gaga, in her videos, situates herself constantly on the boundary of various oppositions – confusing the boundaries of human and non-human, sexy/distorted and ironically exaggerating female objectification so that ribs and spine are on display – in order to question whether all 'male gaze' looking is a distortion. Gaga's clothes always exaggerate 'normal' ideas of fashion and of sexual power and subordination, perhaps critiquing the history of gender oppression through/by fashion. But, crucially, with regard to Butler's theory, is it entirely possible to read Lady Gaga as just 'sexy'? Is the idea that the images in her videos simultaneously reinforce powerful and oppressive ideas about what women's bodies are 'supposed to' look like and draw attention to such 'embodiments' of the beauty standard? Bacon et al. speak for Lady Gaga in this analysis:

> Because I don't allow my gender restrictions to represent how I am perceived, I don't have to be the next 'Britney' or 'Christina'. Am I unwillingly objectified? Or am I authorizing my own power? I am both endangered and dangerous. The category of gender is a means of oppression. (Gaga is forced to be a sex slave) The category of gender is a source of liberation. (Gaga sets her captor on fire with her electrified bra). Are you buying into the idea that women's bodies are readily available commodities? Or are you in on the joke?
>
> (Bacon et al. 2010)

Grouping these perspectives together just for a moment, we can say that more complex versions of feminist media theory suggest that either a feminist media text can only be constructed if an alternative set of conventions, structures and discourses are used because the form and discursive framing of mainstream media is in itself a site of patriarchal power, or a feminist politics is best mobilized by working within gender performance, through playful (and powerful) parody, frivolity and subversion.

POSTMODERNIST THEORIES OF POWER

Jean-François Lyotard (1984) and Jean Baudrillard (1998) offer different versions of postmodernism, both of which are easily applied to contemporary media. Their ideas share a view that the idea of truth needs to be 'deconstructed' so we can challenge dominant ideas that people claim as truth, which Lyotard (1984) describes as '**grand narratives**'. In the postmodern world, media texts make visible and challenge ideas of truth and reality, removing the illusion that stories, texts or images can ever accurately or neutrally 'reproduce' reality or truth. So the postmodern perspective on media is that there are always competing versions of truth and reality, and postmodern media products will engage with this idea.

Two important postmodern ideas are that 'truth' and 'reality' are constructions and that media *re*presentations are actually constructions (presentations of reality, or our idea of it). It is important, during a discussion of powerful media to deal with the central critique of Baudrillard's position – that it's a luxury, available only to people who live in advanced, rich nations and democratic states to take this 'playful' stance on matters of truth, whereas people living through the 'Arab Spring' or the wars in Iraq and Afghanistan cannot afford such a frivolous disposition, given that crucial matters of truth justice and human rights are contested on a daily basis. Either way, a key distinction between postmodernism and the more 'emancipatory' grand narrative theories such as Marxism, is that a postmodernist approach cannot seek to expose and destroy one version of the truth and replace it with a 'correct' one. Another key argument against postmodernism is that the alternative to a belief in truth is relativism – whereby 'anything goes', leading to moral chaos and ethical anarchy.

Returning to the more basic idea that there is no longer a distinction between reality and its representing image, or 'simulacrum', Baudrillard introduced the idea of '**hyperreality**', claiming that Disneyland is the best example we can think of for understanding how our reality works in the postmodern world – a place which is at the same time a real, physical space but also clearly a fictional, representational world. For postmodernists, we inhabit a world made up wholly of 'simulacra' – simulations of reality bearing no relation to any 'real' reality, the idea of which is replaced by the hyperreal where any boundary between the real and the imaginary is eroded.

While Baudrillard was writing his theories with regard to television and cinema, many academics and media commentators see the Internet as having 'realized' some of his postulations (along with those of McLuhan, as we have discussed). While Henry Jenkins does not describe himself as a 'postmodernist' or name Baudrillard as an influence, there are some observations here about 'convergence culture' that would appear to resonate with a 'Baudrillardian' view:

> We are entering a period of prolonged transition and transformation in the way media operates. Convergence describes the process by which we sort through those options. Audiences, empowered by these new technologies, occupying a space at the intersection between old and new media, are demanding the right to participate within the culture.
>
> (Jenkins 2006: 24)

The 'basics' of postmodernism are very straightforward. If people tend to think of media as being 'in between' us and reality, hence the word 'media' and the idea of 'mediation', the postmodernist 'shift' is to observe, or argue, that in a media-saturated world, where we are immersed in media constantly, 24/7, always connected while on the move, at work or at home, then any distinction between 'actual' reality and the (**virtual**) media representation of it is now at least fuzzy, blurred or at most even entirely lost to us. In other words, we no longer have any sense of the difference between real objects and experiences and images or simulations of them. Media reality, or virtual experience, is the new reality. Some see this as a historical development – this has happened 'after' the modern period. In this understanding, artists in the modern era experimented with the representation of reality, and the following postmodern period, which we are living in, is one where reality and representation get completely 'remixed' through pastiche, parody and inter-textual references – where the people that make texts deliberately expose their nature as constructed texts and make no attempt to pretend that they are 'realist'. Others say that postmodernism is not a temporal phenomenon, not a time period in history, but just a new way of thinking.

> The mass media ... were once thought of as holding up a mirror to, and thereby reflecting, a wider social reality. Now that reality is only definable in terms of the surface reflections of that mirror. It is no longer a question of distortion since the term implies that there is a reality, outside the

surface simulations of the media, which can be distorted, and this is
precisely what is at issue.

(Strinati 1995: 224)

In relation to the analysis of media power, the postmodern position
would tend to take individual 'micropolitics' as the norm, and would
certainly resist such 'grand narratives' as Marxism and feminism – as
these offer up an alternative way of seeing the world and seek to
expose the falsity of dominant ideologies currently holding sway. A
postmodern view of contemporary media sees a breakdown of the
distinctions between producer and audience and the boundaries
between people in time and space. But, despite allegations of an
'apolitical' stance, the work of Jenkins, cited above, might offer a new
way of looking at postmodern political engagement.

Jenkins describes 'knowledge communities' and 'textual poachers' –
consumers, critics, fans coming together and falling away from one
another, generally online, in acts of interpretation, a world of
hybridity – old and new media converging. Although Jenkins does
not explicitly adopt a postmodern approach, his work is perhaps the
most obvious example of contemporary media theory connecting
some of the ideas put forward by Baudrillard (writing before the
internet) to current examples of texts and audience behaviours,
framed by his interest in the idea of 'participation culture', which is
the key political theme in his work. After discussing the kinds of
concentrated media ownership which we have discussed, in terms
of their significance for the distribution of access, influence and
power, Jenkins (2006) suggests that 'convergence culture' complicates
this picture in ways that might be 'democratizing'. To make his
point, he discusses the 'digital watercooler' as collective intelligence,
audience backlash against *American Idol* mobilized by an online
'Vote for the Worst' campaign, digital transmedia layering as an element of mass media diegesis; the uneven relationship between the
'folk culture' of fans (now more explicit and 'knowable' in digital
space) and 'big media' producers, peer learning in affinity spaces
and the ways in which participatory culture reworks political campaigning. All of these 'case studies' reaffirm a notion of a shared
public 'mediasphere' but Jenkins suggests a paradigm shift to a new
order of uncertainty over public–private sphere culture. In this
sense, we can see some of the key postmodern ideas – that things

are all 'mixed up' and that politics will become 'micro' – small scale struggles rather than grand 'teleological', revolutionary projects, with an emphasis on 'guerrilla' tactics, as well as the more obviously technologically determinist ideas about how broadband Internet 'affordances' are making all this possible.

POLITICS 2.0? THE INTERNET AND DEMOCRACY

Dixon (2011) describes 'Politics 2.0' as 'the idea that social networking and e-participation technologies will revolutionize our ability to follow, support, and influence political campaigns'. If this is to be realized, then the 'technologically determinist' ideals will need to be realized in sustained evidence of information democracy (unfettered information construction and dissemination), democratization of decision-making (e-democracy) and generally more engaged (in politics) citizens. In other words, a new kind of public sphere, that might be evidenced so far by online polling, blogs and public opinion fora, whereby ultimately the web itself becomes the medium for political action and activism. As always, there is conflict of opinion on all this. Whereas Rheingold (2003) finds 'smart mobs' organizing and mobilizing, coordinating and collaborating online and Lievrouw (2011) identifies the Global Justice Movement as one such organization, Morozov (2011a) labels online politics such as this 'slacktivism'. At the micro level, the '2.0' advocates herald the way that campaign groups create online tools that enable users to send readymade messages to politicians while the critics point out that this is merely spam to their recipients. Similarly, while the current UK government struggles to define its conservative 'Big Society' agenda, it starts to point to social media as a catalyst and Lanier (2011) sees Web 2.0, despite the bold claims, eroding individual identity. For Hindman (2006), it's the claim that Internet politics engage the hitherto disengaged that comes under attack:

> All that happens in online discussion of social and political matters is that college-educated professional, established journalists, commentators, politicians, organisation and think-tanks get a boost to their visibility.

> (Hindman 2006: 24)

The counter-arguments to the 'cyber-utopians' go further, and suggest that the web is increasingly used for surveillance and control *of* the people *by* the powerful and that, under scrutiny, the same people who decry moral panics about 'harmful' media use are actually constructing a mirror-image of such an argument in reverse, by overstating the 'positive' outcomes of media engagement. In reality, they say, most people use the Internet for sex, shopping and entertainment, which suits governments and the rich and powerful very nicely. Returning to 'hegemony', whereby the powerful manufacture consent and attempt to colonize and control any potential sites of resistance, sceptics hold up Obama's use of Twitter to launch his 2012 election campaign, attempts by the Chinese government to control online access and free speech (and Google's complicity in this) and evidence that the US Central Command have purchased fake online identities for propaganda and 'counter-terrorism' purposes – the term for these is 'sock puppets'. Although we ought to pause to consider the fact that this kind of 'control 2.0' is a response to the fact that social media software can be used both for and against the powerful, a state described by Shirky (2011) as 'the dictator's dilemma'. For example, the Sudanese government set up a Facebook group calling for a protest against the Sudanese government, naming a time and place, and simply arrested all those who attended.

Further evidence of 'control 2.0' – the binary opposite of the 'we media' claims for a more democratic online world – is provided by Facebook's storing and selling of personal data, GPS companies doing the same (offering the police data to 'trap' speeding drivers), iPhone's tracking software and more broadly the use by police and security forces of 'Geotime', which captures an individual's movements and communications with other people on a three-dimensional graphic. But on the other side of the coin, there is ample counter-evidence of subversive use of the Internet – from 'culture jamming' (subversion through popular culture in the form of 'memes') and hacking, citizen journalism, 'mediated mobilization' (collective action re-orientated) and 'commons knowledge' (open, crowd-sourced collaborative media content).

Naughton (2010) suggests that the best way for media academics (and students) to sharpen their thinking in order to account for these changes is to resist any notions of 'paradigm shifts' (when one way of thinking ends and another begins) but instead try to conceive of the relationship between media and people as 'ecological'. Going further, he describes 'informed bewilderment' as the best mindset for the contemporary media student. This confusion is created by a combination of mainstream journalism occupying/sharing the 'blogosphere' and the kinds of 'remix culture' Jenkins describes that lead to new forms of value and thus shift the economic basis of media production and consumption. In this environment, media producers have to adapt to survive, argues Naughton, hence his metaphor of the 'ecosystem'. This is a very striking endorsement (Naughton is a journalist) of the 'people power' view of new digital media – that the media industries are adapting to survive in the wake of citizen participation.

On the other side, Morozov (2011a) attacks the bold claims made about the political power (for citizens) of the Internet, and in particular social media such as Facebook and Twitter. Morozov argues that Internet freedom is an illusion, and that technology has not only failed to protect people's rights, but is even used against them by authoritarian regimes, through censorship, surveillance, propaganda and hostility to dissent (the other side, of course, of Chomsky's 'manufacturing consent'). Arguing that the 'cyber-utopian' view is both naïve and a 'mis-reading of history', Morozov views it as a quasi-political form of technological determinism, the view that technology in itself can lead to, or be a catalyst for, political change. Perhaps most bluntly, Morozov reminds us that, despite the great claims made for the power of social media in Iran and most recently the 'Arab Spring', Twitter and Facebook played a minor role compared to mainstream media agents such as Al-Jazeera and, at the time of writing, the powerful have yet to be been overthrown in those places.

In a documentary series screened by the BBC in the UK, Adam Curtis attempted to trace current ecological thinking on 'crowd sourcing' and the democratization of media to the science of cybernetics combined with research into ecosystems and feedback loops in the 1960s. Curtis goes as far as to suggest that current ideas about the Internet's resistance to orthodox power hierarchies are part of a broader shared vision of a 'non-political management of society':

In the mass democracies of the West a new ideology has risen up. We have come to believe that the old hierarchies of power can be replaced by self-organizing networks.

(Curtis 2011)

This is surely an overstatement, but Curtis is more balanced in his critique of the bold claims made for the role of social media in revolutions and general counter-cultural activity:

I'm not criticizing the Internet or Facebook or Twitter. In their main manifestations – the distribution of information – they're wonderful, fantastic. What I take issue with are cyber-utopians, who I think are mind-crushingly naïve, who see democracy as simply you, me and millions of other individuals connected together. And somehow if we could have perfect connections we could organize everything perfectly and there wouldn't be any need for power. Facebook or Twitter can tell you where to join up and rebel but it doesn't allow you to envisage another kind of world.

(in Forrest 2011: 23)

There is a crucial distinction in Curtis' quote above. Democracy is more complicated than mere 'connectivity'. So one mistake the **'we media'** advocates might sensibly be accused of making is to confuse the two, or to assume that one equates to the other. This would make no more sense than to say that the telephone had been in itself a democratizing technology. So, when looking back at McLuhan's famous maxim – 'the medium is the message' – the key issue for media students is to gauge the degree to which the technology/ medium in itself is determining social action.

Buckingham (2010b) is equally sceptical about the power of new media to change the ecosystem in any profound way that we might consider politically important:

To a large extent, the most active participants in the creative world of web 2.0 are the 'usual suspects'. Indeed, if online participation is as socially, culturally and politically important as the enthusiasts suggest, it seems likely that, far from liquidating social inequality, it might actually accentuate it.

(Buckingham 2010b: 6)

Furthermore, 'social media politicians' are now commonplace on Twitter especially, as are political 'apps' for mobile devices and YouTube campaigning. 'If you can't beat them, join them', on one level, but more sinister hegemony on another?

Perhaps it's just a matter of which examples you choose to prove your case. And, as we have discussed, there is a sense here that Media Studies is drifting into the study of, well, everything – the law, politics, social policy, technology and human rights. On the one hand, it's an enormous challenge to respond to such a far-reaching set of questions, but on the other, at least it makes the idea that it's a 'soft subject' even more ridiculous. In a nutshell, in a chapter on media power, the key question is this – to what extent do you think that social media has eroded the gatekeeping model of political information flow? And that is a 'weighty' question.

This, then, is an area where there are no right answers, a debate requiring, from the media student, balance, detail and informed, critical judgement.

CASE STUDY: WIKILEAKS

Whether Wikileaks is a media text or not is a matter of debate, but for our discussion in this chapter, it is certainly of great interest since it's an example of free media and democratic investigative journalism 'par excellence' but as it is not constructed as conventional journalism, analysing it with the key concepts of Media Studies is more difficult:

> One of the main difficulties with explaining Wikileaks arises from the fact it is unclear – and also unclear to the Wikileaks people themselves – whether it sees itself and operates as a content provider or as a simple carrier of leaked data. ... One could call this the 'Talibanization' stage of postmodern – 'Flat World' – theory where scales, times, and places have been declared largely irrelevant. What counts is the celebrity momentum and the amount of media attention.
>
> (Lovink and Riemens 2010: 2).

If, as the saying goes, you've been 'living in a cave', Wikileaks is an international non-profit organization. Ironically, it isn't a 'wiki' in the strict sense, but it is a website that publishes submissions of private, secret and classified media from anonymous news sources, news leaks and whistleblowers. In October 2010, it published Iraq War Logs (400,000 documents), in coordination with major commercial media organizations (including *the Guardian* newspaper), in November 2010, it put out the US State Diplomatic Cables and in April 2011, the Guantanamo Bay files. All of this information has been kept under strict secrecy by governments, but claims that this represents a huge shift in power to the citizen must be kept in check by the fact that in every case, the 'mass' dissemination of the information exposed has been managed by mainstream media, rather than citizens accessing and digesting the cables for themselves.

Shirky (2011) argues that Wikileaks has 'created a new media landscape' and supports the site's founder Julian Assange's very bold prediction that we will come to talk about state power in pre- and post-Wikileaks terms. Morozov (2011b), meanwhile, brings to the surface the irony in the site's name, since a wiki is founded on the basis of shared, non-hierarchical knowledge whereas Wikileaks is biased towards leaked material from elite people and various kinds of experts.

In the end, the barometer is whether the informed media student believes that there should be a tipping point, where freedom of information and the accountability of those in power (going back to Tony Benn's key questions) must end and 'security' begins. This dilemma is neatly summed up here by Jemima Khan:

> Wikileaks offers a new type of investigative journalism. I have my doubts about whether some cables should have been leaked – for example, the list of infrastructure sites vital to national security – and I share the concern that diplomacy could suffer as a result of others. But I feel passionately that democracy needs a strong and free media. It is the only way to ensure governments are honest and remain accountable.
>
> (Khan 2010: 25)

MEDIA REGULATION

Media regulation relates to power in various ways. If we accept that media is powerful, then regulating it is necessary in terms of reducing influence and 'effects'. Media can be regulated in terms of its content or its ownership and distribution. Media regulation is, of course, a kind of power – there are laws that prevent journalists, for example, from reporting some things. And 'the media' would like to see more regulation of 'social media', of copyright and of intellectual property.

Key issues for students of media to explore are:

* How media regulation now is different to how it was in the past.
* How different kinds of media regulation all seek to 'protect' people in some way.
* The degrees of efficiency and impact of various forms of media regulation (how well do they work, and what difference do they make to people's lives?).
* Debates around the role of the regulator in a democracy – arguments for and against various forms of media regulation.

The press (newspapers) in the UK regulate themselves and as a result press regulation is considered 'light-touch' in comparison to other media regulation. If members of the public do wish to take action, feeling that regulations have been infringed, then they can turn to the Press Complaints Commission (PCC), who are considered by some to be a weak body due to the fact that some newspapers perpetuate the practice of 'publish and be damned' in the comfort that they have far more money to use in a legal battle than the individuals who may sue them have. This way of working is described by critics as 'power without responsibility'. The PCC code of practice gives guidance rather than rules with regard to accuracy, right to reply, distinguishing between fact and comment, privacy, harassment, misrepresentation, chequebook journalism, intrusion (into grief or shock), the identification of the relatives or friends of convicted criminals, the protection of children, confidentiality and the definition of 'public interest', which is highly subjective. Investigative journalism into potential corruption by a government minister is clearly in the public interest, but the invasion of celebrity privacy might well not be. On the other hand, editors would argue that if we buy the papers then we demonstrate 'public interest', end of story. The 'Ryan Giggs affair' and the phone-hacking scandal, discussed earlier in this chapter, hinge on these debates.

Shortly after the debates mobilized by the Ryan Giggs case, the role of self-regulating (but, as a result, routinely labelled ' toothless') Press Complaints Commission was thrown into more public and political debate by the revelations that journalists had used illegal and highly unethical phone-hacking methods to mine private information, including tapping the phone of a missing (and later found murdered) schoolgirl, this giving false hope to the parents that she might still be alive. The PCC was criticized from all corners of the debate, most notably by the UK Prime Minister David Cameron who immediately called for a new regulatory system. It should be noted, however, that Cameron himself was at the centre of the scandal, having employed as Press Secretary one of the key figures in the phone-hacking practice.

However, while it might seem 'obvious' that the PCC should be replaced with a tougher external regulator, it is very important that critical media students spend some time considering just how important this protection of the 'free press' is in a democracy. If we regulate the press more than we do at the moment, then we make it easier for people to use their power for unfair ends. The press are free so that they can monitor and report to the public on matters of national interest. In countries where the state owns the media, there is no expectation among the public that they will get anything other than a version of the truth circulated by those in power. So, a 'free press' is a cornerstone of democracy, along with a free vote in a secret ballot and public information being available. Conflict of interest is avoided in a democracy and there is no greater conflict of interest than powerful people owning media and avoiding regulation. The argument – should we have more regulation of the press? – is illustrated by these conflicting statements:

> No commission funded by the newspapers upon which it adjudicates, and working to a code produced by the very editors liable to censure, can possibly inspire public confidence. Self-regulation is toothless.
>
> (Jeremy Dear, National Union of Journalists)

The Press Complaints Commission doesn't impose fines or indulge in histrionics, but it has steadied press standards of behaviour over almost two decades now. It's part of the landscape, increasingly referred and resorted to. And it works alongside the law, not in opposition to it.

(Peter Preston, former *Guardian* editor)

Regulation and freedom of the press is one area among many that are of importance for media students. Others include attempts to regulate the Internet and social media, the classification of video-game content, film censorship, the regulation of advertising and the protection of children from media influence through the facilitation of 'media literacy'. All of these attempts to regulate media are sites of conflict over media power, participation and equality.

CASE STUDY: TALENT TV AND DEMOCRACY

Celebrity culture is said to be the zeitgeist (spirit) of the times. It is seen as significant because it appears to have established new cultural values not present in previous periods. Depending on your view it can either be a form of democratisation or a symptom of cultural decline.

(Helsby 2010: 64)

This section is about the relationship between democracy, interaction and *The X Factor*. It considers the power acquired by Simon Cowell and the extent to which it matters. If, as many argue, Nick Clegg is Deputy Prime Minister in Whitehall largely due to his polished appearances on the 'Cowell-styled' Live Election Debates and the use of social media as an 'extra-textual' feature, then media students do need to make sense of the connections between seemingly more serious questions of media and democracy (phone tapping, ownership, 'we media' in Libya) and issues of access and accountability in apparently 'lighter' examples: the Susan Boyle debate, for instance, was her rise from obscurity to global stardom the American Dream ideal – liberal democracy in action – or exploitation (or both)?

This area of Media Studies tends to be looked at from the perspective of reality television's popularity, cultural value and contribution to forms of realism. Is it democratic and interactive, as the likes of Peter Bazalgette will claim, when he compares young peoples' willingness to interact with the programme by voting and their disinterest in formal politics?

> The discourse of authenticity (who is a 'real' person) and transparency (being 'seen' to be who one says one is) may well offer significant clues to Big Brother viewers' reasons for distrusting and disengaging from politics.
>
> (P. Bazalgette 2005: 281–2)

Or is reality television attractive, in comparison to politics, because it is interactive but not necessarily democratic?

In 2012, 'talent TV' has taken over from 'reality TV' and we are now more interested in the rise and rise of *The X Factor* and all things connected to Simon Cowell. When the 2010 UK general election campaign was dominated by live TV debates connected to social media, the comparison to a 'talent contest' was much discussed and Simon Cowell was given serious credence for his revelation that he was looking at producing a kind of *X Factor* for politicians – maybe by the time of publication this has happened. Along with 'talent TV' – a wide range of programmes where contestants compete over several weeks in particular contexts, from *The Apprentice* to *The Choir* – there has been a proliferation of 'reality documentaries' where elite people or celebrities are placed in unfamiliar and threatening situations. *Tower Block House of Commons* and *Rich, Famous and Homeless* both put celebrities 'in the mix' with 'real people' for the vicarious pleasure of the viewing public. Comic Relief in 2011 extended this further by placing pampered celebrities in the slums of Kenya.

Finding a space in between the 'difficult' theory and seemingly 'easy' subject matter ('talent TV'), this is the perennial conjuring act for media students. In this case, a contemporary application of Adorno's theory of the 'Culture Industry' (Adorno and Horkheimer 1973) is helpful to provide a theoretical framework for these questions about the 'power' of *The X Factor*:

> The culture industry perpetually cheats its consumers of what it perpetually promises.
>
> (Adorno and Horkheimer 1973: 139)

Adorno's work is a good example of the 'coming together' of analyses of political economy and ideology. According to this thesis (from the Frankfurt School of critical theory), the effect of both ownership and textual content is to standardize commodities, culture and, in effect, people. At its most cynical, popular culture is viewed as exercising social control:

> The culture industry serves the ideological interests of economic and political powers by producing music, films and other sentimental novelties designed to make people cathartic, amused, satisfied with their lot, sleepy and, after a good night's sleep − re-charged for tomorrow's chores and the office, farm or factory.
>
> (Laughey 2007: 124)

In this way, looking at **Frankfurt School** thinking as a development of Marxism, the shift is to see popular culture as the obstruction to a revolution, as opposed to physical power and religious or educational ideology. Of course, it is only possible to agree with this view if we: a) see people as completely 'passive' in their reception of popular culture; and b) see popular culture as formulaic. Most contemporary media theory has moved a considerable distance from these perspectives.

Adorno's analysis was profoundly negative, but his theoretical desire was to expose the contradictory and illusory nature of popular culture in its status as a commodity 'for sale' masquerading as something external to economics. There was, in his view, very little difference between art and advertising, but the producers of the former were mystifying their actions in order to preserve a false distinction between these activities. Culture is always for sale and is, indeed, produced for that purpose and so the idea that we can escape from the daily workings of consumer capitalism through enrichment by culture is a myth. The clearest connection between Adorno's work on popular culture and Marxist theories of power is in the idea that popular culture has a distracting function in the way that it presents the idea of the talented, or cultured individual when, in reality, that individual is merely a part of the capitalist system and is dependent on it. Adorno didn't see anything 'trivial' in the role of popular (or 'mass') culture, though:

Although life in the capitalist democracy of America was a far cry from Nazi Germany, Horkheimer and Adorno did never-theless find similarities between the two contexts. The experi-ence of American cinema and commercial radio confirmed Horkheimer and Adorno's view that 'enlightenment' had turned into 'mass deception' through the machinations of 'the culture industry'.

(D. Barlow and Mills 2009: 184)

While it's important to carefully state at this point that no con-nections are being made between Simon Cowell and Hitler, it's nonetheless apparent that some of these ideas about entertain-ment as 'deception' are applicable to *The X Factor*. Cowell's creation would, in Adorno's terms of reference, be an example of 'mass cul-ture' (or 'anthropological culture') compared to, say, the novels of Ian McEwan. Adorno's view was that high culture does have an emancipatory potential, through being in some ways 'outside' of the everyday processes of economics and administration – 'material life', but its form is conservative and not politically progressive, since it caters for those that are already favoured by the system. Popular culture, though, is the opposite – potentially revolutionary in its appeal to 'the masses' who are alienated and repressed by those in power, but in its form and content this kind of culture is absolutely part of the machinery of the system – not only does it 'commodify' culture to the extreme, it also serves to distract 'the masses' with its superficial, 'accessible' content. Thus Adorno presents the paradox at the heart of 'the culture industry':

The critical energies in the elite concept of culture had to be marshalled against the ideological function of its anthro-pological counterpart, while the progressive impulses of the latter had to be turned against the conservative implications of the former.

(Jay 1984: 115)

Turner (2010) describes the proliferation of 'ordinary people' on television in the 21st century as a 'demotic turn' and his view is different to Bazalgette's in that this is not the same as a demo-cratic shift. The cult of celebrity, for Turner, creates a new set of expectations of everyday life, so the ordinary person is not featured in the media on 'ordinary' terms:

> No amount of public participation in game shows, reality TV or DIY celebrity websites will alter the fact that, overall, the media industries still remain in control of the symbolic economy, and that they still strive to operate this economy in the service of their own interests.
>
> (Turner 2010: 16)

Once again, then, there is a question with no 'right answer' to be posed – does the attention to the 'ordinary person' by television actually constitute a revolution in the eroding of boundaries between elite and everyday, or is Turner right when he argues for attention to the more orthodox power dynamics 'behind the scenes'? Turner's argument is that there is no clear connection between the exposure given to 'everyday people' by reality TV and any kind of progressive or emancipatory shifts. Thus the 'demotic turn' equates merely to the increase in exposure of/to the public with no necessary democratic outcomes. Furthermore, he suggests that the rise of celebrity culture – and with it the clamour for us to seek the prize of commodifying ourselves as celebrities has had the effect of charging the contemporary media with the power to 'translate' cultural identity.

Is it possible to connect Marx, Adorno, Cowell and Turner in this way? Adorno, of course, was writing in a very different period and he was primarily concerned about the distracting nature of jazz! In addition his problem with 'popular culture' was not intended to be elitist. But what would Adorno have had to say about Simon Cowell, and would he have agreed with the idea that the Internet creates democratic 'affordances'? That is highly unlikely. For certain, the relationship between 'talent TV' and democracy must be located within a very complex field. The crucial thing is to connect the 'light' and the 'heavy', to understand that Simon Cowell's (unelected) power, Murdoch's (recently compromised) agenda for UK domination and the affordances of Twitter by people in Egypt fighting for liberation are connected – the culture industry is very different now to when Adorno was writing, but the relationships between culture, media, everyday life and power are the same.

POWER AND GLOBALIZATION

The next chapter provides an introduction to theories of global media. There is a clear overlap with this chapter, because a contemporary analysis of media power must grapple with the relationship between 'state power' in a particular nation, ways that global communication across borders will offer resistance and opportunities for power to be exercised globally. So global media is always the subject of debate and there are examples of all three of 'people power', ideological power and corporate power being increased by new digital media that transcend traditional boundaries of time and space. More basic theories of global media argue that McLuhan's 'global village' prophecy is being realized as we move away from ideas of local culture, reinforced by such media as local news and radio, towards a sense of ourselves as global citizens. Marxist perspectives on this thesis vary, but the idea of 'cultural imperialism' connects most clearly, whereby the ideas of powerful nations (most commonly the US) are spread around the world to the extent that a 'cultural empire' is created through the virtual invasion of American ideas into the cultures of nations across the globe – not only does this mean that we expect to find a McDonald's or a Starbucks in every town but also that we come (in the UK context) to understand ideas about the world from America as 'closer to home' than those originating in other parts of Europe. It is, as always, much more complicated than that, and the 'right answer' tends to be that examples of global culture co-exist with people retaining local identities and that global media often 'culturally mutate' to become hybrids of the global and the local – 'glocalization'. Furthermore, there are a plethora of well researched and documented examples of '**diaspora**' – a term describing the process by which people disperse themselves across the world and take elements of their media culture with them, the popularity of Bollywood cinema in many parts of the world being a key 'case study'. All of which is stated to remind you that, as we move from theories of media power to global media, the key questions about the role of media in society are common to both areas of study.

SUMMARY

This chapter has introduced you to a range of different but related ways in which media can exercise power over citizens. At the same time, a range of examples of citizens using media (especially new social media) to challenge power or exercise power of their own have been discussed. The key theoretical ideas for studying power in / by media – Marxism, cultural imperialism, political economy, feminism, postmodernism and the more recent idea of 'Politics 2.0' have been described, and the most compelling 'no right answer' debates have been introduced – the degree to which we are 'passive' recipients of media ideologies; the dangers to democracy that media ownership can present; the need for more or less media regulation and the potential of new social media to facilitate a new 'non-political' ecosystem.

The ideas and examples covered in this chapter can lead to the following summative statements:

* In a democracy, citizens are entitled to a free media, with open access and impartial information flow without gatekeeping, but media analysts and commentators rarely find this in practice.
* Power can be with or without various kinds of accountability and it is important for citizens to ask questions about the accountability of media owners and producers.
* Marxist analysis of media power attempts to reveal the ideological nature of media texts, whilst discourse analysis attempts to trace the intertextual framing of political media discourse.
* Feminist media theory is varied and changing, but a common thread is the analysis of seemingly neutral media as gendered, with the male point of view as 'the norm' and thus power is exercised through the construction of female as 'other'.
* Postcolonial media theory looks at the ways in which physical empire-building (by military conquest and invasion) has been replaced by ideological empire building, partly through the spread of dominant media across national and cultural boundaries.
* Postmodern media theory foregrounds mediation and challenges the notion that media represent any separate, prior state of reality. Media power can be amplified or fragmented in this model as 'grand narratives' (such as Marxism or Islam) are apparently replaced, for many, by single issue, short term 'micropolitics.' Much of what is happening with social citizen media – for example in the 'Arab Spring' – appears to support this thesis.

* There is great debate and disagreement over the potential of an online, mediated 'Politics 2.0' to lead to a new 'non-political' democracy.

FURTHER READING

All of the work referred to in this chapter is listed in the bibliography at the end of the book, but the key recommended reading on the material covered in this chapter is as follows:

Barlow, D. and Mills, B. (2009) *Reading Media Theory*. Harlow: Pearson.
Contains a range of 'classic' examples of theories covered in this chapter, with a critical reading of each.

Davies, N. (2009) *Flat Earth News*. London: Vintage.
Award-winning 'expose' of biased, unethical and corrupt journalistic practices.

Morozov, E. (2011) *The Net Delusion*. London: Allen Lane
Argues that claims that the internet has enhanced democracy are ill-founded.

Oates, S. (2008) *An Introduction to Media and Politics*. London: Sage.
Covers news production models in depth.

Turner, G. (2010) *Ordinary People and the Media: The Demotic Turn*. London: Sage.
Distinguishes between interactive, democratic and demotic.

4

GLOBAL MEDIA

AIMS

This chapter will introduce you to:

* International approaches to studying media;
* Theories of globalization and of global media;
* The role of social media in constructing a 'global village';
* Cuba as a rich case study for international/global media analysis.

There are two ways in which your study of media will need to take a global perspective and these are separate but related areas.

Firstly, an international perspective on 'world media' takes you out of the comfort-zone of only studying media that is circulated in your country. So, depending on where you are, this might mean that you develop a case study on Hong Kong cinema, videogame reception in Mexico or Internet access in Cuba.

Secondly, a consideration of theories of global media requires an understanding of the ways in which capitalist market forces, changes in audience behaviour and new technologies combine to increase international media production, distribution and reception.

But these two study areas are brought together by a focus on the issue of media and identity – how do media representations and exchanges reinforce, challenge or negotiate new elements of local, national and global identities?

> The meeting of the global and local is a meeting of integration and co-existence, and not a choice between two contradictory opinions. It is a dialectic process of 'push and pull' between the two poles.
>
> (Lemish 2006: 216)

INTERNATIONAL MEDIA STUDIES

Examples of an international perspective are, of course, almost infinite, so we can only cover a few examples by way of suggesting an approach for adaptation.

African hip hop radio is a cross-media case study that allows for the consideration of media conventions, audience, the relationship between promotion and critique and the interplay of local, national and international subcultures. Perullo and Fenn (2007) describe a filtering process whereby young people in Malawi and Tanzania channel North American hip hop styles through their own local musical, linguistic and social environments but in different ways (thus avoiding a reductive model of an 'African' response without local difference):

> Both countries have vibrant hip hop communities that draw on youth knowledge of international, as well as local and national, hip hop music and culture. Youth in the two countries listen to the same popular American stars and hold similar opinions about and interpretations of their lives and music. Yet Tanzanian and Malawian hip hop scenes diverge in the social and cultural significance of local music practices, which include performing as well as dancing, dressing and talking about rap music.
>
> (Perullo and Fenn 2007: 19)

The researchers go on to describe this as 'the tension between the similar and the different'. This way of looking at global media is a view we will return to throughout this section.

Media exchange in and between Arab nations is of great contemporary interest to the media student. In particular, the way that news events are reported by Al-Jazeera, compared to the Western representations of the same events, alongside attention to the use of social media by participants in the 'Arab Spring', will take us into big questions of power and ideology. At the same time, a study of video channels in Arab nations reveals some important developments in cultural transformation – around **hybrid** identities and claims and counter-claims about the power of television channels to undermine or fragment youth identity in highly patriarchal Arab societies (Hafez 2008).

A study of the 'telenovela' in Latin American nations can provide a rich analysis of reception in relation to cultural identity and gender in particular, either as a 'stand alone' international study or in comparison to soap opera reception in the UK or US. The dual function of the telenovela as entertainment and a form of 'social education' is often described as 'pro-social media' but a student of media would need to look at reception in order to assess the **ideological** implications of such media that 'prescribed a variety of roles for women both in the domestic and public sphere where they enjoyed a certain empowerment and agency, were simultaneously keepers of local religious and cultural traditions, spoke up to male miscreants, and yet deferred to strong males in their social contexts' (McMillin 2007: 89).

Research into cinema in New Zealand provides an interesting consideration of how 'Global Hollywood' (Goldsmith 2010) interrelates to ideas of unique 'kiwi culture' that, in turn, must be understood in the context of New Zealand's origins and separation (physically) from the rest of the world. At the micro level, an analysis of the work of cinematographer Al Bollinger – most notably portrayed in the documentary film *Barefoot Cinema* (see McDougall and Smythe 2010) – can set up an international perspective on production, distribution and reception of a national cinema that oscillates between the 'internal' representation of itself and the commercial appeal of film that it understandable to global audiences. In this sense there are obvious comparisons with UK cinema.

You will notice that each of these suggestions for an international media case study or research project almost immediately expand into bigger critical questions about power, representation and identity. For that reason, you should never think about a study of world media as being simply the acquisition and demonstration of 'key facts' akin to a geography project on another country. The factual basis – historical, economic and political – will be very important, but the critical media student will then connect this understanding of how media work in different locations to the 'macro' themes of the subject. No case study more clearly connects the micro to the macro than Cuban media, and this chapter concludes with a more detailed investigation in that area.

GLOBAL MEDIA BUSINESS

Whilst some aspects of **globalization** may be new – most notably those enabled by digital technology – media have been globally produced and distributed for a century at least and increasingly consumed across national borders for all of that time. The story of globalization is, perhaps ironically, the story of concentrated ownership, with this international spread of media leading to fewer, not more, companies from fewer, not more, countries dominating media industries. At the same time, pinning down the national origin of a media product is very difficult in the age of global convergence:

> A production might be financed globally, written by writers in Los Angeles, filmed in Vancouver and Australia, acted by Europeans, and distributed worldwide.
>
> (Press and Williams 2010: 168)

In a detailed case study on *Slumdog Millionaire*, Branston and Stafford (2010: 163) argue that the film can easily be understood as a 'global text' because it was adapted from an Indian novel in English, filmed in India using a local crew managed by UK professionals, sold for distribution to a range of international companies including Fox (it is argued that this had a profound impact on the global reach of the film and its subsequent acclaim) and the film featured a score by one of Bollywood's most famous composers. Branston and Stafford suggest that *Slumdog* is neither purely British nor a Hollywood or a Bollywood product, but it has benefitted from being perceived as each of these. Academically, the debates over its significance relate more to the accusations of 'cultural tourism' (a Western view of the Indian 'other'), which are countered by those that acknowledge the way that the film is partly constructed within the conventions of Indian cinema.

GLOBAL CITIZENS

One problem with theories of globalization, which critical students of media need to carefully sidestep, is that they have tended to polarise the debate. On the one hand, theories of **cultural imperialism** construct America as an all-powerful, invading force, spreading its values and commercial imperatives all over the planet – the McWorld idea. On the other hand, there is a more positive account of cultural hybridity and 'glocalized' media, whereby we 'mash up' cultural styles, mixing the local and the global and thus becoming more cosmopolitan – this view of the 'glocal' sees globalization as a force for good in the development of cultural diversity. As usual, the reality is probably a bit of both.

In 1960, McLuhan's *Explorations in Communication* introduced the idea of the 'global village'. As we have already discussed in relation to the claims for online 'people power', there is a view that McLuhan was something of a prophet, writing as he was before the networking and connecting affordances of digital media, before mobile phones even. McLuhan is hugely important for Media Studies still for the precise reason that he predicted the process of globalization as the product of society being increasingly 'mediated'. Globalization could not work without people being more aware of global culture, and this happens through the media, in this sense globalization is an incremental process as people get more and more exposed to more and more media that does not originate in their own country. Robertson (1994: 41) adds a more distinguishing account of this process as 'both the compression of the world and the intensification of consciousness of the world as a whole'. Here, the two separate but mutually dependent elements of the 'global village' are described. Understood in this way, we can see that it is only possible for us to read, view, download and buy products (media content and everything else) that are produced abroad if people know they are there for us to access.

> In a globalized world there will be a single society and culture occupying the planet ... it will be a society without borders and spatial boundaries. We can define globalization as a social process in which the constraints of geography on social and cultural arrangements recede and in which people become increasingly aware that they are receding.
>
> (Waters 1995: 3)

This definition situates globalization geographically. If this view is accepted, then, as you become increasingly global in your outlook, you will care less about your local or national culture and identify with more agreeable, aspirational and cosmopolitan values and ideologies, to the extent that you will come to see yourself ultimately as a 'global citizen'.

This is a contested viewpoint. Moores (2005) argues that our idea of the specific place, the local, is not 'marginalized' (made less important) by globalization, but is instead made 'instantaneously pluralized' (Moores 2005: 66) – in other words, we just visit (virtually) a lot more local spaces rather than one big virtual global space. This is a simple but very important distinction – plurality (less of more) versus hegemony, an idea we have come across several times in this book (more of less). Moores writes about the scenario whereby you are walking around a city talking (via technology) to a friend in another country. In a sense, in this example, you are in two places at once, simultaneously local and global.

> Globalization divides as much as it unites; it divides as it unites – the causes of division being identical with those which promote the uniformity of the globe. What appears as globalisation for some means localisation for others; signalling a new freedom to some, upon many others it descends as an uninvited and cruel fate.
>
> (Bauman 1998: 2)

THE PUBLIC SPHERE

Habermas (in D. Barlow and Mills 2009) provides us with a model for understanding society as being the meeting point of individuals in the 'public sphere' and much 'mass communication' theory that informs Media Studies adopts this view. In the public sphere, individuals can meet, interact and have an impact on politics in various ways. While metaphorical – so it can expand to online, virtual 'spaces' – the public sphere is visible and, for the most part, civic. Habermas's view is largely optimistic about the degree of agency individuals can have in a liberal democracy, and as such media models of mass communication that draw on Habermasian theory tend to see mass media as providing a space for interaction and expression. So, the commentators and academics who see the Internet as

democratizing are likely to adopt such a position. This is complicated by globalization, as it is much harder to say what the public
sphere is and where a national public sphere would end and a
global space would begin, or whether the Internet simply provides
us with a global public sphere. Theorists of global media tend
to suggest that we are departing from models of the 'nation state'
and towards a notion of there being various levels of public
spheres – a more horizontal arrangement. The interplay between
'mass' television and more fragmented media engagement online
illustrates this shift.

At the end of the previous chapter we set up global media as part
of our exploration of 'powerful media'. Less than 20 per cent of the
human race have broadband Internet access, so how 'universal' can
global media be, if it is determined by technology and access to it?
Bauman sees 'winners and losers' in the process, reminding us of the
crucial fact that more people are excluded from the 'global village'
than are included – rather a contradiction in terms, you might well
think. Is it the case that in the global media world, powerful groups
of people share ideas, exchange trade, buy and sell and dominate
markets of various kinds. And if this happens, is it true that for the rest
of us who are 'left out in the cold', our local cultures are marginalized
and undermined?

Although the new electronic networks have partially replaced the relatively stable and enduring traditional communities with which we are
accustomed, they also facilitate countless highly specialized social and
cultural connections that otherwise would not take place. Millions of
people all over the world are taking advantage. As technological and
cultural landscapes evolve, the sense of belonging and community does
not disappear; it changes shape.

(Lull 2006: 56)

Lull's more complex and less polarized account sets up some more
important 'no right answer' areas for students of media to explore. How
are specific areas of the media changing to become more 'globalized'
in terms of how media is produced, distributed and exchanged? Who
are the 'winners and losers' in this and how will these transformations
impact on ideas about culture, community and society?

While we need to be careful about the kind of 'technological determinism' that assumes that networked digital media is a panacea for everything, Media Studies academics do tend to agree that global media has become much *more* of an issue for debate since broadband became accessible for the public on a mass scale in developed nations. But it's vital to challenge any idea that media used to be national and now it is global, as though this is a neat, linear, historical development. As Hartley (2007: 63) reminds us, 'globalization is as old as the media themselves'. That said, Web 2.0 is – with a few interesting and important exceptions such as China's restricted version of Google – essentially a global network for the exchange, consumption, critique and adapting 'by the people' of information, knowledge and media content. At one end of the continuum, major corporations such as CNN, Apple and the BBC use the Internet to reach wider audiences than previously possible. At the other end, children share videos on YouTube and get gratifying (or not) playback from viewers anywhere on the planet. The first kind are organized, commercial, corporate and strategic. The second are examples of 'we media' – organic, random, creative and much harder to analyse. Irvine (2006) explains global digital media's potential to transform the social world in this way:

> At the extreme, modern media simply dissolve time, distance, place and local culture that once divided the globe. Perhaps the best examples are computer games and pop videos. Routinely their content blurs boundaries of history and geography in a mix that denies the specificities of actual locations and particular chronological periods. In effect, we are putting all our cultural eggs in one basket.
>
> (Irvine 2006: 5)

While Irvine seems to take a negative view of global media, there being an inference in this statement that perhaps geographical and cultural boundaries are important and their erosion is damaging, others celebrate the 'shrinking world', for the more 'feelgood' emancipatory and environmental reasons that Gauntlett (2011a) offers and on perhaps colder, economic grounds. Financial meltdown notwithstanding, it's much easier now to disseminate cultural products across the world, to travel on cheap flights to connect with people abroad in the physical world and to use technology to do the same in the virtual domain with citizens from all nations.

Resisting the temptation to over-generalize about 'global culture' is really important for students of media. The 'interplay' in people's lives (including your own) *between* the local and the global is what is under the critical lens. While a simplistic (and easy) approach is just to declare that global media dominate our lives and we get all of our cultural reference points now from those powerful corporations who have managed to distribute their media products worldwide and thus 'mediate' us, there is always resistance to this. Equally, wherever you are reading this book, your own perspective is not universal – there are many countries where global access is limited, either for political, economic or cultural reasons. In these societies the nation-state, controlled by the government, will still be far more central to mediation. So you need to locate your own reading of global media theories in relation to the local and national context for your own mediation. There are many societies in which religious faith competes with the 'pull' of Western media. So a media student should be 'examining globalization processes from the ground, from the level of lived experiences' (McMillin 2007: 180).

It should be clear by now that you are encouraged to avoid simplifying global media. Just in case, Stafford provides this synthesis of the ideas we have encountered so far:

> Globalisation is not simply the West expanding uniformly, in a 'blanket' way, into the rest of the world. For one thing, other countries' media forms have exchanges with, and even flow into and out of, 'the West'. Words like 'flows', 'networks', 'corridors' and 'transnationalisation' have tried to signify this more complex mapping. They try to suggest that when we talk of media 'covering' territories, there are always gaps and spaces in that only-apparent 'blanket' coverage.
>
> (Branston and Stafford 2010: 148)

POSTCOLONIALISM

This theory is shared by all disciplines with an interest in texts and culture (English, drama) and by social sciences such as history and philosophy. The name can be misleading as it does not assume that colonialism is a thing of the past. Far from it, the theory looks for evidence of colonial operations being translated/transformed from physical military invasion, conquest and occupational rule to a cultural equivalent – the invasion and occupation of culture, whereby dominant nations impose 'their' value system as the 'norm' and marginalise local difference as 'other'. Media are not the only agents of this, but they are important in the equation.

As we have seen, Media Studies is about connecting the seemingly trivial and everyday landscape of 'low culture' with 'big theory'.

POSTCOLONIAL THEORY IN ACTION

To further demonstrate how postcolonial theory operates, there is no better example than Paul Gilroy's (2004) analyses of Mike Skinner (The Streets) and Ali G. Gilroy suggests that Ali G's repertoire of irreverence is underpinned by 'an antipathy toward the stupefying US styles and habits that have all but crushed local forms of the black vernacular and replaced them with the standardized and uniform global products of hip-hop consumer culture' (Gilroy 2004: 147). The claim here is that, despite 'relativist' or even 'cultural year zero' appearances, the construction of Ali G is a warning to youth in the UK that the violent, capitalist excesses of the global hip hop 'franchise' are not accessible to marginalized urban youth in Britain and so the absurdity of the character's posturing is not only satirical but also directly political – not intended as a celebration of the hegemonic cultural signification at work. In simpler terms, this means that, underneath the comedy is a serious point about young people being manipulated by a seemingly global but in many ways exclusive set of meanings being distributed from the US. Ali G is subverting, mocking but at the same time challenging these ideas about 'global culture' by showing how awkward the 'fit' is between the global mythology and the local context. In a very different analysis of popular culture through the lens of postcolonial struggle, Gilroy locates in the music of The Streets an attempt to think through Britain's national history and to (along with Billy Bragg's reconstruction of a non-racist patriotism) create a 'playful ontology' in which the Americanized trappings of globalization can be resisted. In this vision, 'race is not an identity that can fix or contain individuals' and:

> This little England certainly owes something to its nativist predecessors. It certainly shares their commitment to the relocalization of the world,

but it has expanded their horizons and overcome their xenophobia. Racial difference is not feared. Exposure to it is not ethnic jeopardy but rather an unremarkable principle of metropolitan life. Race is essentially insignificant.

(Gilroy 2004: 105)

In looking closely at Ali G and Mike Skinner, Gilroy allows us to see the complexity of the situation and this attention to the awkward, complicated detail is the key criteria for critical study of media. Ali G is not appropriating or affirming the mainstream hegemonic 'repackaging' of potentially radical hip hop culture. On the contrary, the satire can be read as resistance to it in the 'local' UK context. At the same time, The Streets are *reformulating* another kind of resistance to globalization but in a multicultural context without stating it as such – indeed, by reducing race to the margins to reframe postcolonial Englishness as very different to the US but also very different to previous visions of 'Little Britain'. In both these examples, we are forced to resist the binary opposition approach to globalisation through which we would be tempted (because it is easier) to define media examples as either proof of or proof *against* the rise of global media. Both Ali G and The Streets, according to Gilroy's reading, subvert this way of understanding global/local cultures by 'reframing' the boundaries between them.

DIGITAL POSTCOLONIALISM

A constant theme in this book is the extent to which the Internet can be seen to transform relationships between media producers and audiences and to connect people in new ways so that alternative forms of, and remixing of, media can be generated. This has obvious implications for postcolonial theory because there are two co-existing possibilities – that the 'globalizing' force of the Internet will increase the domination of powerful cultures over their 'others' and that the peer-networking affordances of online media can provide more opportunities for people to reinforce and renegotiate their marginalized cultural identities:

The possibilities for challenging dominant ideologies implied by collaborative technologies and independent online publishing concur with postcolonial commitments to challenge the centre from the margins. Digital reading practices defer authority to a reader or to multiple readers and in general terms have a tendency to question the authority of a text and its author. Clearly this has direct parallels with postcolonial endeavours.

(Ramone 2011: 199)

When studying global media, paying attention to the rhythmic differences between media use and function in different countries is essential. British youth enjoying the frivolity of Ali G is a different 'case study' to, for example, the potential of new social media to offer a space for postcolonial identity in authoritative regimes is the subject of much current research. For example, Suwito (2011) investigates expressions of national identity on Facebook in Indonesia. Suwito's research suggests that Facebook allows a space where people can express opposition to authoritarian regimes, observing that:

Facebook functions to reconstruct the postcolonial identity by means of narrative in marking the transition from colonized subjects to liberated beings. Facebook provides a mechanism to formulate a 'new' community that hold power to form a collective struggle of those who were considered as the 'other' – the ones formerly excluded or marginalized from the oppressive discourse. Certain ideas are liberally spread out in Facebook, creating an unstoppable flow of resistance toward the dominant discourse and changing the face of the nation.

(Suwito 2011: 25)

So, comparing the examples of research and academic analysis above, we can see clearly that avoiding generalization is crucial in any consideration of global media.

HYBRIDITY

The most basic understanding of hybrid identity suggests that, instead of thinking of the cultural identities of people in far-away locations as isolated from one another, we should consider them to be interrelated and complex. For example, dominant Western media formats that are successful across the globe achieve this power precisely because they are adapted into the 'cultural idioms' of various locations and, as such, hybrid forms of texts and, more significantly, hybridized acts of reception form a majority, when taken together as a whole. This idea has been marginalized in Media Studies. In its clearest manifestation, a hybrid TV format is franchised across cultural and national boundaries with adaptations to accommodate local cultural differences. These alterations will have the double-effect of reducing offence and increasing the audience. *Who Wants to Be a Millionaire?*, which has been broadcast in Korea as *I Love Quiz Show*, in China as *The Dictionary of Happiness* and in India as *Kaun Banega Crorepati*, most notably the subject of *Slumdog Millionaire*. Formats that require little in the way of adaptation are 'culturally transparent'. Another format that required significant 'local differences' is *Survivor*. When imported to Hong Kong, the programme shifted its focus from competition between contestants towards collaboration, reflecting the very different political, cultural and moral context.

Perhaps the most striking example of a 'glocal' hybrid programme is the Beijing domestic drama *Joy Luck Street*, based on *Coronation Street* but with a great deal of cultural adaptation.

Life on Mars, in its original form, relied on an understanding of English policing over several decades. However, distributors were able to export the same show to Canada, France, Germany, the Netherlands, New Zealand, Australia and Finland and adapt it for the US (Los Angeles) and Spain (Post-Franco, 1978). Going the other way, *Dragon's Den* originated in Japan as *Money no Tora* (Money Tiger). The UK, Australia, New Zealand, Canada and the Netherlands all use the same title but in Israel people watch *Hakrishim* (Hebrew for 'The Sharks') and in the US, *The Shark Tank*. We might reflect here that the programmes that are the most 'culturally transparent' are those that share an economic-moral modality (competition, ruthless business). In this context, *The Apprentice* is another highly formatted export. A franchise that originated in the US in 2004 hosted by business tycoon Donald Trump, the UK version hosted by Lord Alan Sugar has needed very little 'local translation' in one sense, but the iconic tasks, judges and settings often act as a showcase for specifically UK elements of 'rags to riches' capitalism. Similarly, the show has seamlessly reached mass audiences in Germany as *The Big Boss* and in South Africa, India and in Arabic nations with similar titles and famous tycoons firing and ultimately hiring.

There is, then, a distinction to be made between hybrid pro-grammes where specific cultural adaptation is required and transparent exports where the format stays in place but names and presenters change. The former complicate theories of globalization, while the latter can be used as evidence of the 'global village', perhaps.

> Hybrid programming becomes a key strategy in the latter domain, to meet the rising demand for programmes that contain elements of the global, yet are charged with local relevance in terms of language, themes, actors and contexts. Hybrid programming allows lighthearted combinations of global and local programming elements. The average consumer is able to appreciate the humour in the caricature of both global and local and recognise his or her membership in a media world that transcends national borders.
>
> (McMillin 2007: 112)

GLOBAL NEWS

The five leading providers in global news are Al-Jazeera English, with 100 million viewers globally (but not in the US); France 24, with French and Arabic versions; CNN, (double Al-Jazeera's audience and presenting an explicitly American news agenda); Russia Today, often state-biased, according to commentators but never conceded by the organization itself; and BBC World, viewed by analysts as the most impartial. Each has a global news agenda with a national origin.

News is usually included prominently in any study of global media because citizens tend to be more concerned about the status of their news provision than what they perceive, rightly or not, to be 'just entertainment'. The public in the UK have largely accepted Hollywood domination of cinema in terms of what is screened in cinemas and broadcast on TV/available for legal on-demand viewing. But if UK news came directly (and visibly) from America, this would be less palatable. Likewise, the rise of user-generated content on YouTube is, for most people, an interesting new form of media that sits alongside commercial film and television, while citizen news – eyewitness journalism and blogging by 'Joe' – provokes debates about accuracy and bias, and also the law. Wikileaks is a unique case, but the arguments over freedom of information versus public interest resonate with the attention we pay to news as a fundamental element of citizenship, so where it comes from and who produces it tends to be of more pressing interest than the origins of music, videogames or magazines. Hartley has developed a model of online journalism that takes us beyond territorial boundaries (where news is distributed from and to) to a consideration of transformations of 'news time':

> Traditional journalism and broadcasting have pitched their tent, as it were, in the temporal rhythm of the day and the week. But this is the frequency that seems the most under attrition in the present developments. There may be a challenge to traditional daily/weekly journalism and broadcasting in this scenario. People are responding to different speeds of public communication, but this doesn't necessarily mean the end of democracy. It's not dumbing down but speeding up.
>
> (Hartley 2007: 53)

According to Rosenberg and Feldman (2008: 35), our expectation of a 'global appetite for speedier news' was fuelled by the First World War but has been more recently satisfied by technology with the result that our desire for instant, constant and global news has undermined serious journalism. Once again, they evoke the fast-food giant in labelling this 'McNews':

> New media are producing and nourishing a Google generation of information consumers – those who want news fast, so they can receive it without breaking stride the way a marathon runner grabs a cup of water on the run. And hitting the refresh button won't change the way these people think.
>
> (Rosenberg and Feldman 2008: 24)

Returning to the question of space for a moment, the increasingly global distribution of news, due to the emergence and success of a small number of global news services is a trend that has been labelled 'CNN-ization'. In simple terms, the American news network, along with Sky, Fox and the BBC, circulate news using satellites to geographically diverse and in some cases remote parts of the Earth. So if we continue to look at news as a locally or nationally produced service, which we have tended to, then we are trying to cling to the idea that stories are selected and constructed in relation to a particular set of news values that are generated by editors' assumptions about ideas about what audiences in regions and nations are entitled to be informed about or are likely to be interested by. If news is produced far away from where it is received, then questions of news agendas – what is selected and constructed, for whom and for what purpose – are more complicated.

THE BBC

The BBC's international news services attract a global weekly audience of more than 200 million people. BBC World – the commercially-funded international English language news and information television channel – has estimated audiences of almost 80 million viewers a week. The corporation's online news services attract around 40 million unique users in any one month.

According to Global News Director Richard Sambrook:

> The BBC's news services are strengthening their impact with audiences around the globe in the highly competitive multimedia age. People around the world are increasingly turning to the BBC when they need quality news and information that is independent and trusted.
>
> (BBC press service release, 21 May 2007)

AL-JAZEERA

Al-Jazeera's news agenda is clearly stated and transparent – to use the same global strategies employed by Western corporations in order to challenge the news agenda offered by them. Al-Jazeera English (AJE) has the objective of counterbalancing the 'global news supremacy' exercised by the likes of the BBC, Fox and CNN but in so doing the network is critical in its treatment of Arab governments as well as American foreign policy. The global appeal of AJE resides in its status as alternative to both Western and Arabic news offerings. Critics would argue that news hegemony operates so powerfully that only the most 'media literate' citizen is actually able to make such an informed choice, and in reality most people assume their news is reliable, honest and transparent.

The thoughtful audience member would hopefully watch Al Jazeera and other broadcasts like CNN and BBC. The way to counteract bias from one program is to not rely on just one source of news. In the past, the Arab and non-Arab audience had little choice, however, but to listen to either Western-dominated news with its particular bias, or to receive news of the Arab world from Arab regimes. Al Jazeera has offered a revolutionary alternative that has helped to create a new Arab discourse and alter the Arab media experience. It is obviously biased, but it does present an Arab perspective in a world where Arab voices were not particularly distinct.

(Al-Jenaibi 2007: 2)

News is, then, a 'global commodity' and as such it is bought and sold. News agencies such as The Associated Press, Reuters and World Television News supply international news (they claim) as 'pure information' so the news agenda of the reporting organization is 'applied' to the raw data. However, you won't be surprised to read that analysts and academics take a sceptical view of this and argue that, although the news agencies do not explicitly share the news agendas of the Western networks, because they know that Fox, CNN, Sky and the BBC are their main 'clients', they will provide news that they perceive to be 'customer facing'. If that's the case, then news provision becomes circular, and the concern is that non-Western events are marginalized by never even becoming news.

DIASPORA

Diaspora describes the dispersal of people around the world and the ways in which audiences take their media with them:

Diasporic audience research emerges from the fact that the media's role in cultural mediation is influenced by the movement of people as well as goods. The vast audience for Indian and Chinese media, in its various dialects, exists on an international as well as national level.

(Ruddock 2007: 72)

This is a serious challenge to the 'cultural imperialism' theory that would appear to assume that American media in particular will reduce any attempt to cling to any notion of cultural heritage through media consumption. A range of studies describe ways in which media reception can be a feature of hybrid identity formation – people using media from their heritage cultures alongside their home nations as part of a 'management' of their identities.

Academics developing research in the area of media globalization are usually agreed on the importance of **ethnographic** research methods. These methods involve spending time in the social context of the audience group being researched in order to 'go native' and get to grips with the specific local context as far as possible, to bear witness to the interplay between the local and the global rather than assuming that everyone is experiencing the media in the same way in some idealized 'global village'. One example is provided by Durham's research (2004) into teenage girls of Hindu cultural heritage living in Florida, who were using the media partly to construct a 'hybrid' identity. Durham discovered, through the ethnographic process, that the female participants were making use of *Friends* in conjunction with Hindi films to 'switch and splice' two aspects of their identities, as described by Ruddock (2007):

> Both of these experiences were meaningless on an explicitly textual level; *Friends* was just 'stupid', where Hindu musicals probably mean something, but the girls did not know what. But on a cultural level, both resources helped the girls mediate the different worlds they inhabited; *Friends* accessed a high school [language] where musicals contained a sense of Indianness shared with parents. The girls found themselves being Indian in Florida due to forces beyond their control. They had to figure out what this means, partly by using media products made by multinational systems of production and delivery. But it was up to them to make these power dynamics real by embodying them in specific ways.
>
> (Ruddock 2007: 71)

Studying media demands attention to such specific 'embodying of cultural meaning'. It's not about understanding globalization merely by imagining that everyone attaches similar meanings to the same cultural artefacts. Rather, it's to do with understanding meaning-making in global contexts as a vast array of 'small stories' – rather than a simple 'grand narrative' of cultural imperialism.

To further complicate things, when global framing is used to construct local meaning, this is referred to as 'glocal media'. Thussu (2007) refers to such complexities in terms of 'global flow and contra-flow'. Put simply, once the idea of global culture becomes systematized, then any manifestation of local identity is already positioned in a global context. Bollywood is, again, invoked here – being at once internally referential (patriarchal and concerned with Hindu identity-struggles) and equally framed by global anxieties (pan-Asianism, Americanization, cultural imperialism). Global flow, then, describes the circulation of media from dominant nations (normally North American), while 'contra flow' describes the processes by which local identities act to divert or re-channel the flow.

THE GLOBAL CHILD

Despite all the rhetoric about the role of the Internet in global media trends, research into 'global childhood' often locates television at the centre of this, with particular attention to the dominance of American television in children's media consumption. The implications of this are that when television arrives in a country it brings with it 'an entire value system and political economy that are quite often foreign to the receiving country' (Lemish 2006: 213). We have already encountered the McWorld thesis and this dystopian vision is most striking when focused on the commercial corruption of childhood. In this alarming scenario, children are lured into a world of Americanized values and aspirations.

> Children all over the world sing similar pop tunes, wear similar clothing and drink the same soft drinks. Can we argue that they are living in a shared global culture? As a result, do they perceive the social world in similar ways? Is their local identity being erased? Are they evolving the same vision of themselves as consumers, individuals and citizens of the world?
>
> (Lemish 2006: 214)

The key distinction is around the extent to which 'global' means American. Is global culture a neutral, international space or just a global rolling-out of American values as apparently (especially to 'innocent' children) neutral and international? Either way, where the adult world view television as potentially harmful, the antidote is often prescribed in terms of education (media literacy) or parental control – Sue Palmer's *Toxic Childhood* arguments centre on televisions in bedrooms. The irony here is that, while for some the Internet is even more of a problem (if parents have a struggle controlling television viewing, this is nothing in comparison to monitoring online activity), for others (such as Gauntlett 2011a and Wesch 2009) the Internet offers a more interactive liberation from the passive 'sit back and be told' culture that television fosters, a state that Postman (2006) famously described as 'amusing ourselves to death'.

As always, while the concerns over children in the global media landscape are most compelling when they are grounded in evidence of the commercialization of childhood, the situation is far more complicated, in terms of both the way that TV programmes are produced and their reception. Lemish (2006) looks at *Sesame Street* from a global perspective, describing its popularity with children in almost 150 countries (more than 120 million global viewers) and the way in which, in 20 countries, its production is collaborative (between its US originators and broadcasting institutions in the 'host' nations) with the effect of a hybrid version blending the 'standard' content with locally created elements. *Sesame Street* has an explicitly educational agenda and there is evaluative research to prove its success in this regard, but the demographic analysis of this shows that children from disadvantaged backgrounds watch the programme less frequently than their more affluent (in economic and cultural terms) counterparts. This research turns the 'Toxic Childhood' and the 'McWorld' arguments upside down and compels us to look in more detail at the content of television. Furthermore, researchers suggest that the 'glocal' nature of *Sesame Street* is one of the main reasons for its educational successes:

> When children in various countries are exposed to watching co-productions of the original program, they are exposed to a program with the original American features that have proven to be effective that are embedded in a local cultural context, with local educational priorities, a local cast of characters and the like. Thus, for example, the Chinese program devoted a section to aesthetics deemed missing from school curricula, special attention was given to the transition to an open society in Russia;

an attempt was made to deal with the Israel–Arab conflict in the Middle East and mothers were addressed in an effort to eradicate illiteracy in Turkey. This approach of combining local cultural content and the Sesame Street format is said to be at the heart of the program's unprecedented international success.

(Lemish 2006: 176)

The critical media student will be drawn here to questions of power and hegemony, even while acknowledging the positive role this programme may be playing in global education. The critical questions would be most substantial and challenging with regard to the transition to capitalism in Russia and the representation of Israel and Palestine. What is the balance here between neutral, global space for education (Habermas's public sphere) and American ideology, which is far from neutral with regard to Russia and the Middle East? Are children engaged in an open space for considering these conflicts and changes, or is there a 'manufacturing' of children's consent?

Buckingham (2007, 2011) adds analyses of Pokémon, Disney and Harry Potter to the mix. In the case of Pokémon, the cultural imperialism and glocalization theories are 'muddled' by the fact that Pokémon is, in fact, an 'Americanized' adaptation of a Japanese product, enjoyed by children for its 'cool' and 'exotic' connotations but also transformed through a 'deodorizing' process whereby a measure of what might be 'too Japanese' is used and elements that are viewed this way are transformed into more American features (Buckingham 2007: 50). In the case of Harry Potter, Buckingham sets up critical questions which are as yet unanswered but might hold the key to understanding globalization:

What it is that Chinese children, whose lives are very different in many ways from those of children in Britain, seem to recognise in Harry Potter? Does this point to the existence of some kind of universal, global child-hood – or is it that these texts are interpreted in such different ways in different cultures that they effectively become very different things?

(Buckingham 2007: 52)

Buckingham (2011) also outlines the increasingly global market for children's television and the way that this might undermine the negotiation of local and national identities in the texts that children engage with. At the same time, he draws attention to the way that the campaigning discourse is bound up with broader ideas about cultural values and hence there is an assumption that children will be better educated by television that represents their own culture, and this will have a more positive impact on their identity formation and contribution to citizenship, but there is no real evidence for this.

CASE STUDY: MEDIA IN CUBA

Why is a study of Cuban media useful in the context of globalization? Because it spans both approaches – Cuban media, by virtue of being in an economically challenged communist context, is unique, so the international perspective is clear, a comparison of Cuban media with any other nation will yield rich data to 'theorize'. At the same time, the complexity of Cuban media in terms of democracy, access, inclusion and regulation is striking and this connects the 'micro' detail to all of the 'macro' themes explored in this chapter.

Firstly, a brief history of politics and economics in Cuba – these are crucial to frame the study. Cuba is a communist state and understanding its place in global politics and culture is complicated. On the one hand, educational and medical provision is the envy of most countries but on the other, trade restrictions mean that material possessions are scarce and the infrastructure of the nation is crumbing. Lambie (2008) describes Cuba's place in the world 'against the grain' of much analysis by arguing that it is global capitalism that is fragmenting and Cuba exists as a vital counter-hegemonic alternative. The argument here is that the current economic crisis allows us to see Cuba in a new light:

> By looking at Cuba, not in isolation from the world, it questions how its 'unity of purpose' can continue to influence and be absorbed into the growing popular resistance movements emerging within the core of 'globalisation'.
>
> (Lambie 2008: 139)

This interpretation challenges the dominant discourse that casts Cuba as a unique, socialist 'red herring' in the course of global capitalism and instead claims Cuba as a surviving alternative to a failing economic system. Famously, in the aftermath of the Cuban revolution, Fidel Castro declared that his leadership of the coup would be 'absolved by history' and clearly Lambie finds evidence of such exoneration in current global struggle. However, any serious exploration of Cuban media needs to look into the relationships between state ideology, public sphere responses and private concerns – most notably evident in new digital spaces. Lambie writes about 'influences that are diluting the revolution' and clearly new social media, alongside a tradition of counter-cultural cinema in Cuba, can be cited as such.

To visit Cuba is to witness confusion and contradiction on every level. Literacy levels are the highest in the world and citizens are proud of free healthcare, but a sense of time warp pervades. Richard Gott, one of the county's most notable commentators, describes the experience:

> I found a Cuba preserved in aspic: nothing seemed to have changed – one of the unique and neglected charms of communism. An intelligent, healthy and well-educated population, younger than the revolution itself, survived in buildings battered by time, with rations that were barely adequate, and with a transport system that did not serve their needs. They had plenty of reasons for complaint, yet they were slow to attack the revolution or its leadership.
>
> (Gott 2009: 1)

The material poverty is the result of trade restrictions imposed by the US. The degree of severity in trade and travel restrictions changes according to the will of presidential regimes – Reagan was very hostile, Clinton tightened the economic embargo but relaxed travel rules and Bush, after 9/11, made the latter much stricter again. Cubans are hopeful that Barak Obama will lift these and recreate commercial relations with the island. At the time of writing, the President had just reduced restrictions on US citizens applying for visas to travel to the island for study.

'Old media' dominate in Cuba, so it is important to look at newspapers, film and TV next. The state-controlled newspaper, *Granma*, named after a yacht that played a historic role in the revolution, is distributed for free on the streets and is available online in translated, international, form. It is overtly and shamelessly a vehicle for **propaganda**. On 22 June 2011, the main story concerned a UNESCO report on children's handwriting that:

> ... 'put Cuba at between first and third place in all parameters' and that 'it can be said that Cuba has very high results in written texts, taking into consideration moreover that the percentage of blank or illegible texts was less than 1% in both grades.'

In television broadcasting, academic debates offer contrasting interpretations of the role of popular soaps (telenovelas) in facilitating public debate about social issues, as opposed to providing another medium for government ideology. For example, *Mulheres Apaixonadas (Passionate Women)* is broadcast three times a week on Cubavisión, one of Cuban state television's four national channels, to millions of viewers. For reasons that shed some light on freedom of speech in Cuba, it is argued that the social issues covered in telenovelas could not be freely discussed by Cubans otherwise:

> Although this is a country with excellent laws that protect women in their relationships, there are still many deeply rooted patriarchal customs. These serials serve as spaces for bringing up subjects like violence, lesbian sexuality, alcoholism and others that we don't know how to approach otherwise.
>
> (Acosta 2008: 1)

BUENA VISTA SOCIAL CLUB

The film *Buena Vista Social Club* and its soundtrack offer, for many, an iconic version of Cuban culture and provide, for analysts, a rich example of a hybrid media form – American producer Ry Cooder reconstructing the ensemble from original members of the pre-revolutionary club (what are the political implications of an American intervention of this nature?). What the club represents is important in the context of Havana as a 'signifier'. An African-Cuban venue, the *Buena Vista Social Club* hosted a range of converging musical styles – mambo, jazz, rhumba and son montuno and charange, cha-cha-cha and pachanga dance movements to choreograph the sound. As such we can see in *Buena Vista Social Club* the hybridized and even post-modern nature of pre-revolutionary Cuba, and this offers a rich comparison with more contemporary musical subcultures.

CUBAN HIP HOP

Guerrilla Radio – The Hip Hop Struggle Under Castro (www.youtube. com/watch?v=e-rDkhIvR_4) is a documentary that seeks to chronicle the battle over freedom of speech in contemporary Cuba from the perspective of DJs, rappers and other musicians. Another example of the complexity of Cuban media and identity, the film explores state suppression of counter-cultural art along with vio-lence towards women and the omnipresence of poverty but at the same time shows that the hegemonic absorption of American hip hop into the mainstream (to the extent that the more 'cutting edge' proponents of the form no longer manage to influence the culture, it is argued) makes Cuban hip hop a more radical space – an 'explosion that's just started', as one young rapper in the film describes it. In this way, the potential for political and cultural change in Cuba – and the extent to which the people desire it – is often presented as being within the power of the 'next generation' and there is a perceived interplay of youthful radicalism and tech-nological progress that can facilitate this. For example, *Cuba Va* (directed by Dolgin and Franco) is a video-to-film transfer that presents a complex view of the island directly from the perspective of young citizens with contrasting opinions:

What they have to say or sing or rap suggests that everyone born after the revolution has an opinion, and those opinions are diverse. What it also suggests is that father Fidel, whether he intended to or not, has produced an extraordinarily articulate generation that defines itself through political positions. Here is a nation in which young men and women believe that their personal behaviour has a public meaning and consequence and that even being alienated is an act of social rebellion. The one area of agreement among those interviewed is the wish to be left alone after Castro's departure to sort out Cuba's future.

(Kardish 2004)

Figure 4.1 Cuban Semiotics

CUBAN CINEMA

Another important film for addressing complex and diverse opinions
and identities among younger Cubans is *Strawberry and Chocolate*
(directed by Tomás Gutiérrez Alea and Juan Carlos Tabío) that represents sexual discrimination at the end of the 1970s. The interesting
'angle' here is that the director Gutiérrez Alea is a committed
revolutionary who wishes to explore critically the double standards

of the post-revolution society 'from within'. The lead character is eventually forced to leave the country despite being firmly committed to the political project of the revolution, simply because of homophobic persecution. The fact that the film is celebrated within Cuba as a triumph of state-supported film-making (the directors were supported by the Instituto Cubano del Arte e Industria Cinematograficos) indicates the complicated nature of contemporary public sphere identity-politics. To illustrate this, posters of the film are sold to tourists in the gift shops and hotels of Havana while gay people in the country are still subjected to discrimination in formal political society – indeed, Castro has declared that homosexuals cannot be accepted as members of the revolutionary Communist party and this approach is, according to West (1995) a 'dark stain' on the history of the revolution. *Strawberry and Chocolate* is a film which attempts to represent the 'identity crisis' of post-revolutionary Cuba in symbolic ways, as this extract from an interview (from the film journal *Cineaste*) with Gutiérrez Alea shows:

> *Cineaste*: One of the central themes of the film is the question of Cuban identity. Would you comment on the Cuban altar in Diego's house and the film's use of Cuban music?
>
> Gutiérrez Alea: That altar, which was in the short story, defines Diego's personality very well. Diego is enamoured of Cuban culture. This aspect of his personality makes the ending of the film – when he must abandon his country because he cannot live out his potential fully – all the more dramatic.
>
> (West 1995: 18)

Before Night Falls (directed by Julian Schnabel, 2000) offers a more hard-hitting filmic account of prejudice and repression in post-revolutionary Cuba. The film depicts the persecution of exiled gay poet Reinaldo Arenas. There are two ways in which critics see this film as more transgressive and bold than Gutiérrez Alea's text. Firstly, the film is more overtly sexual and adopts the perspective of the 'gay gaze'. Secondly, the film is more visceral and aesthetic, adopting magical realism in a far more straightforward celebration of gay life and condemnation of the Cuban regime, according this reading, from Smith:

> While *Strawberry and Chocolate* is static and earthbound, confined to the apartment where a stereotypical queen and a humourless Marxist

engage in relentless debate, *Before Night Falls* is mobile and volatile. (The producers) have already been bitterly attacked by so-called solidarity campaigns which confuse support for Cubans with support for the regime that has denied them democracy for over 40 years.

(Smith 2001: 31)

GENERACIÓN Y: DIGITAL TRANSFORMATIONS

More than political unrest, economic discomfort or even the death of Castro, the Internet may be the catalyst for change in Cuba. However, it is important to understand the dynamic relationship between three aspects of online activity in Cuba – state use of the Internet for disseminating political messages; state restrictions on Internet use by citizens and citizen media in the forms of blogs which are often counter-ideological or at least critically negotiate the functions of the state.

Turning first to state use of the Internet, Fidel Castro no longer speaks publicly due to failing health but regular 'reflections of Fidel' are provided online for citizens. For example, in May 2011, after the execution of Osama bin Laden, Castro posted an item about 'lies and mysteries' surrounding the events and disseminating the outcomes of various international surveys that suggest there is a great deal of suspicion about the claims made by the US to have killed bin Laden and that a significant number of people do not accept the US position on bin Laden as the mastermind of 9/11. Such 'reflections' are clearly intended to frame international events in the discourse of revolution and to pre-empt Cuban citizens' access to global (and particularly, American) media representations of such events.

In an earlier example from 2010, Castro offered his response to Wikileaks, again with the desired outcome of providing a lens through which Cuban citizens might view this event. Celebrating the roles played by filmmakers Ken Loach and Michael Moore in funding bail for the site's creator, Castro offered this view (translated online by *Granma International*) of the broader political context for Wikileaks:

The motivations which led him to the resounding blow that he delivered to the [US] empire remain unknown. All that is known is that morally, he has brought it to its knees. World opinion will continue closely following everything that happens in the context of Wikileaks. Responsibility for being able to know the truth, or not, about the cynical politics of the United States and its allies will fall squarely on the right-wing Swedish government and the bellicose NATO mafia, who so like to invoke the freedom of the press and human rights. Ideas can be more powerful than nuclear weapons.

(Castro 2010)

Although the island has been connected since 1996, for most people there is limited access to the Internet in Cuba. The reasons for this are a combination of government restrictions, the US trade embargo that means Cuba is cut off from American trade of various kinds (including websites, which are often 'reverse filtered' from the US so they cannot be accessed from Cuba) and lack of finances (less than 5 per cent of the population own a computer). Logistical barriers add to this disconnection – Cuban IP addresses are hard to acquire (from US providers) and bandwidth is inadequate. Those Cubans that can access the web in some form are in most cases restricted (financially) to a national, state-controlled, intranet system. Of course, this information only describes measurable legal use of the Internet but it is worth bearing in mind that illegal use of the Internet, under the umbrella heading of 'counter-revolutionary activity' can lead to 20 years in prison. We can see, then, that the Cuban state's approach to the Internet is far from open and democratic. The Cuban government use the Internet primarily to disseminate political responses to events and also for tourism and the administration of medical services, but on a limited and heavily controlled scale:

Reporters Without Borders considers Cuba 'one of the world's 10 most repressive countries [in regard to] online free expression' because of the highly limited access and the severe punishment of illegal Internet use, including 'counter-revolutionary' usage. The restrictions stem from the strong desire of the Cuban government to prevent attacks upon its political ideology from broad access to contrary views.

(Open Net n.d., accessed 2011)

ELIÁN THE 'NOWHERE BOY'

A rich case study for understanding global media as a site of struggle over truth and origins can be found in the story of Elián Gonzalez (seven years old at the time) who, following the death of his mother who drowned while trying to sail from Cuba to Miami in 2000, became the subject of a struggle between Miami and Cuba over his citizenship. Eventually, he returned to Cuba with his father. According to Allatson (2004), the case became 'virtualized' in the sense that Elián became an icon in popular media culture through websites, books, films, radio shows, art, a *South Park* episode, T-shirts and posters. The central argument is this – the idea of a 'state' is a process of virtual representation manifested in processes of signification over the 'values' of a society, so in this reading:

> Cuba emerges in signifying terms as an illusion with the potential to produce and host Cubanness, as well as rival ideals of nation that can be accessed intact, at will, and ready for ideological deployment. Crude dichotomies of antagonism — Cuba/USA, home/exile, democracy/communism, freedom/tyranny, North/South, godlessness/blessedness, consumption/want — characterize the hegemonic struggle over the Cuban nowhere.
>
> (Allatson 2004: 3)

As Elián temporarily came to exist in a 'nowhere space' in the sense that both claimants denied that the other was a legitimate space for his citizenship, Allatson suggests that the 'virtualization' of Elián is a metaphor for the identity crisis of Cuba in the context of global media. Elián was trapped between two Cubas – the island itself and another version of it in Miami. Cubans in America were campaigning (unsuccessfully in the end) to 'Save Elián' from Cuba itself. This struggle continues online with many of the 'Save Elián' websites (from the US) continuing in order to campaign against Castro more broadly. In Havana, meanwhile, posters can be seen all over the city condemning a US conspiracy of lies in the reporting of the case and celebrating the repatriation of Elián as a 'replaying' of the failed attempt by America to invade Cuba and as such another victory against imperialism. In this case we can find elements of **cultural imperialism,** hybridity and **diaspora**, all mediated across borders:

> In Elián's case, the voyeuristic media-machine attained unprecedented intensity because it met and worked with the virtualities of the Cuban nowhere, part of it in the USA. Thus, a transnational surfeit of Elián-narrative options was guaranteed for participants, audiences and

commentators alike, wherever they resided. In Cuba, Elián was hailed as
the child-hero of the Revolution. In Miami he was a saviour sent by God.
Day by day, Elián's story was propelled across the globe by melodramatic
plot devices familiar to viewers of soap opera.

(Allatson 2004: 5)

The Internet, then, is the site of much political struggle and
attempts to regulate its use are often futile. For these reasons,
commentators on Cuba are keenly 'watching this space' to assess
the potential of radical citizen media to facilitate political change.
Yoani Sánchez is an acclaimed Cuban blogger who produces
'Generación Y' and has been honoured with a Digital Journalism award
by a Spanish organization upholding work in the area of social justice,
which she was unable to collect due to Cuban travel restrictions.
Time magazine named her one of the hundred 'most influential
people' in 2008 (a notable intervention from an American media
institution, for various reasons, if we consider cultural imperialism
and the 'McWorld' thesis). Generación Y is not, however, explicitly
political. Venegas describes the author's work in this way:

Her objective as a citizen journalist is to write from the personal about the
political. Her entries focus on the obstacles of everyday life – inefficiencies,
insufficiencies, infrastructure problems, impractical policies – as well as
conversations with neighbours and fellow bus riders, capturing through
their candid comments the ways that Cubans face difficulties. Her
writing (in Spanish) avoids political rhetoric and reveals that she is not
part of an inner intellectual circle but rather of an independent community of aficionados committed to expanding the content and participation
of media in Cuba.

(Venegas 2010: 173–4)

Despite this subtle approach to weaving the personal with the political, Sánchez is alleged to be the subject of state surveillance and the
label 'mercenary of imperialism', which is used to describe all
counter-revolutionary activists (Sánchez would not accept this
charge). Here she describes the state response to her blog:

The simple fact that I published my opinions and pointed out that all
these organizations did more to control rather than represent us carried
serious consequences. Even now, I can't leave the country. The state is

seeking revenge because I contradicted it. People follow me on the street, watching my every move. My telephone has been tapped. I stopped parroting the government's slogans years ago and I no longer belong to any official organization. I am a free citizen, a free radical. My blog, my political platform, consists of a single demand: the diversity of opinion can no longer be a crime!

(Sánchez 2011)

If this version of events is correct, then this provides an amplification of Castro's assertion that 'ideas can be more powerful than nuclear weapons' but at the same time a profound double-standard that seems indicative of so much of contemporary Cuban politics – powerful ideas are to be liberated (Wikileaks) and suppressed (Generación Y) in equal measure. But Venegas (2010) warns us against viewing the Internet in Cuba from a free market perspective – itself an imperialist approach – and instead suggests we should situate Cuban media in the context of change and complexity, a situation he describes in terms of 'digital dilemmas'. The Internet was, after all, 'designed by the enemy' so the switch from analogue to digital is a different transformation in Cuba:

A new social imagination has begun to shape the future of Cuba, taking it beyond earlier rhetoric even where that rhetoric is digitized.

(Venegas 2010: 184)

CONTROL AND FREEDOM

As we have seen, there is an 'identity crisis' in Cuba and a sense of being at a crossroads. Young people are cited as the agents of change and will play a key role in defining Cuba over the next decade, with students very much in the forefront of developments. As Obama has relaxed restrictions on study visas, it might be possible for students from across the world to be involved in this, as Joan Coatsworth from Columbia University in the US suggests:

Cuba has never been more interesting. Most Cuban students, whatever they think of Fidel Castro or his brother Raoul, and as much as they are proud of their country, are impatient for long-overdue changes. It's an exciting process that students can witness firsthand.

(in Cunnane 2011: 20)

Having mapped out the changing mediascape in Cuba, the final stage in a case study of this nature is always to 'map' this factual understanding to some applicable theories. We have previously engaged with McLuhan's 'global village' idea and, whilst some look back to McLuhan as a prophet of the online age, this case study on Cuba provides an antidote to any reductive assumptions by obliging us to consider the interplay of local, national, global; of personal, social and political and of private and public when we are taking a more **'ethnographic'** view of how people in specific situations might be more or less global in their more or less mediated outlook. Another key theoretical framework for such analysis is provided by Chun (2006) whose 'Control and Freedom' provides a way of balancing the Internet as a control system with the space it creates for personal and political freedom.

> The Internet's potential for democracy stems from the way it exposes us to a freedom we cannot control. Freedom does not result from our decisions, it is what makes them possible. This freedom is not inherently good, but entails a decision for good or for evil. The gaps within technological control, the differences between technological control and its rhetorical counterpart, and technology's constant failures mean that our control systems can never entirely make these decisions for us.
>
> (Chun 2006: 49)

In conclusion to our Cuban case study, Venegas's 'digital dilemmas' chimes with Chun's account in that both help us understand the importance of these 'in between' spaces (in between local, national and global; in between control and freedom; in between private and public and in the case of Elián, in between two versions of an identity). While both argue that the idea of the Internet as a utopian space outside of control is a fantasy, they suggest that this very fantasy allows for different kinds of (more idealist, or optimistic, perhaps) decisions to be made – and as such the illusion of freedom plays an important facilitating role in shaping the future, of Cuba and elsewhere. Critical students of media have a role to play in understanding the complexity of these changes, over time, and must resist simplifying them into generalising binary oppositions:

> Cubans will surely continue to pick the digital locks, perhaps increasingly for personal gain rather than common good, as global

cybercultures creep under the Cuban door carrying new forms of social expression.

(Venegas 2010: 66)

SUMMARY

This chapter has introduced you to the distinction between an international approach to studying media and understanding various theories of global media and suggested that both are essential.

The ideas and examples covered in this chapter can lead to the following summative statements:

* Reductive and simplistic accounts of global media and the effect of this on culture and identity should be avoided. Equally, it must always be remembered, when evaluating theories about technology and global culture, that most of the world's population are not connected to broadband Internet.
* Global media is best understood in terms of tensions, complexities, flow and counter-flow, hybridity and the construction of highly specific 'glocal' meanings which are best understood through ethnographic research.
* It is crucial that the critical student of media explores research evidence for assumptions that might otherwise be made about the effects of 'global childhood' or 'global citizenship', set against evidence of local resistance, Diaspora and 'glocal' counter-flows.
* A case study example such as Cuban media demonstrates the dynamic interplay between media, technology, control, freedom and identity.

FURTHER READING

All of the work referred to in this chapter is listed in the bibliography at the end of the book, but the key recommended reading on the material covered in this chapter is as follows:

McMillin, D. (2007) *International Media Studies*. London: Blackwell.
Full of research-informed material about hybrid media.

Murphy, P. and Kraidy, M. (eds) (2005) *Global Media Studies*. London: Routledge.
Introduction to a global approach to the subject.

Thussu, D. K. (2007) *Media on the Move: Global Flow and Contra-flow*. London: Routledge.
Accounts for the 'fluid' nature of global media and resists binary oppositions between local/global.

Venegas, C. (2010) *Digital Dilemmas: The State, the Individual and Digital Media in Cuba*. London: Rutgers University Press.
This chapter's 'Cuban case study' draws on this book, which explores the complexity of Cuban media in the online age.

Waters, M. (1995) *Globalization*. London: Routledge.
Provides a framework for understanding broader notions of global flow and exchange, which can then be applied to media (and vice versa).

5

CHANGING MEDIA

AIMS

This chapter will introduce you to:

* The suggestion that 'Web 2.0' makes 'Media Studies 2.0' necessary.
* Significant theories of change for critical students of media.
* What Media Studies might look like 'after the media'.

> Media use is quite different for teenagers today by comparison with fifteen years ago. It is clear that media education needs to engage with the changes, whilst still retaining a critical distance on their impact.
>
> (Fraser and Wardle 2011: 545)

So, do we need 'New Media Studies' to do this? In this chapter we turn our attention to a situation Bob Dylan famously summarized with 'there's nothing as constant as change' (Shelton 2003). For the critical student of media, the object of study is constantly shifting. Consequently there is a great risk of any subject matter appearing here being out of date within weeks of publication. For that reason, we won't be taking a 'case study' approach here, looking at particular kinds of technology and the impact they may be having on media producers and audiences. Instead, we will engage with the academic debates and theoretical perspectives on media in the online age. These critical approaches are adaptable and applicable to whatever new forms of technology, media, culture and experience are around the corner.

The history of what we understand as media and future projections for media and culture were covered in length in the first chapter. At this point, we turn to the key critical questions about changing media. To what extent has media production been transformed by broadband Internet? Equally, and importantly, we must consider examples of media that have remained untouched by such developments. What impact does broadband Internet access have on audience behaviour? Or should we be talking about 'the concept formally known as the audience' in the age of the '**prosumer**'? Next, we must carefully map the significance of media **convergence** at the levels of ownership, production and reception. In the era of the iPhone (a computer, telecommunications device, camera, videoplayer, TV, radio and music player), can we distinguish any more between media forms? And finally, critical media students need a balanced, informed view on the competing visions of the future – Media 3.0 and beyond. Some are dystopian, some utopian. A critical perspective avoids binary oppositions and will end up somewhere in between.

Henry Jenkins writes about a 'participatory culture' in which we might have more of a say in public discourse if we harness online tools in the right ways:

> I tend to rely on the various studies done by the Pew Center for the Internet and American Life – especially their recurring estimates of the number of young people who have produced and shared media. Their 2005 report showed that 57 per cent of American teens had produced media content for the internet; by 2007, those numbers had grown to 64 per cent and they have reportedly continued to grow since. These numbers, of course, differ from one national context to the next, but they suggest a significant shift in levels of production and participation from the pre-digital era.
>
> (in R. Berger and McDougall 2011: 14–15)

There are optimistic and more dystopian visions of where all this might lead, of course. Marshal McLuhan's theory that 'the medium is the message' has been, as discussed in the first chapter, the subject of some renewed interest, on the grounds that contemporary social media seems to be making some of McLuhan's predictions 'come true'. Along with the 'global village' (covered in depth in the chapter on Global Media), another key element of McLuhan's work was his observation that 'we shape our tools and thereafter our tools shape us'. Many media academics are looking at the way that our ways of using media are changing as we switch from a television-dominated media environment to an online, connected ecosystem and McLuhan's theory of tools that shape us seems even more credible:

> We wonder whether social networking might be fuelling political revolution. And we ask if Google is making us stupid – or at any rate whether net-worked technology is reducing attention spans, devaluing memory and blurring the line between making online connections and forming real relationships. Over all these contemporary debates looms the shadow of McLuhan, who now seems more insightful than ever.
>
> (Naughton 2011: 19)

CASE STUDY: MEDIA STUDIES 2.0

This idea was put forward by Will Merrin in 2007 and then dis-seminated and expanded by David Gauntlett. Soon after it became the subject of much criticism, most notably from David Buckingham. We won't indulge in too much navel-gazing here, given that this book aims to introduce you to the subject, not unpack it all. Gauntlett's response to his critics will suffice here by way of a summary of the main thrust of the argument:

> A recognition of the straightforward fact that the media landscape has changed significantly in the last 15 years, so that the traditional textbook categories of 'film', 'television', 'newspapers' etc., along with 'the internet' in a parallel but separate category, are increas-ingly redundant, as internet-based technologies are used to blur the range of places where we can encounter, interact with and contribute to media content. The internet has not only become hugely important in itself but has forced all the media around it to change accordingly.
>
> (Gauntlett 2011b: 356)

Buckingham (2010a) had responded to this intervention with accusations of 'technological determinism' and a broader attack on what he calls a 'Californian ideology'. Understood this way, Media Studies 2.0 is an overstated celebration of new media that fails to take into account the political dimensions of corporate ownership, divisions in access and the need for critical analysis of Web 2.0, as opposed to a 'blind' acceptance of its 'affordances':

I would agree that it is necessary to keep pace with our students' media experiences and their changing orientations towards media. Nevertheless, we also need to beware of assuming that those experiences are all the same (the 'digital generation' argument) and keeping up with our students does not mean we should automatically import the latest technological gimmicks into the classroom, let alone start pimping up our Facebook profiles in some hopeless desire to be 'down with the kids'.

(Buckingham 2010a: 26)

However, Merrin's original idea was not about only about Web 2.0 challenging Media Studies to rethink its approaches, but rather he argued that the advent of interactive media more broadly needed to be accounted for, whereas until recently the subject had focused mainly on 'mass media'. This idea takes in much more than just the Internet.

Wherever you stand on this, it's fair to say that Buckingham does 'lump together' some very different ideas in this 'digital generation' accusation and it is important to distinguish between the observation that the Internet (along with other forms of interactive media) has fundamentally altered what we mean by 'the media' and the less robust idea that young people are born **'digital natives'** (from Prensky 2010). The most important element of this argument for critical media students concerns the charge of 'technological determinism, which Gauntlett responds to here:

Technological determinism' is a charge which is often levelled at people who are merely seeking to discuss ways in which technology *could* be used. It's laughable, sometimes – and

> quite intolerable – how an argument which merely dares to suggest a positive rather than negative application of social media is instantly branded as 'technological determinism'. You could say it's part of an academic sickness, that to be seen as 'cool' and 'critical' you can only subscribe to the most negative diagnoses of everything.
>
> (Gauntlett et al. 2011: 115)

On the other hand, C. Bazalgette is concerned with how arguments about participation in the '2.0' era are evidenced:

> I want to know how 'actively shaping' is defined and what counts as an 'active role' in producing, circulating and appraising, and the extent to which this can be teased out from the 'web 2.0' business model. My understanding has been that there's a smallish core of people to whom it would be appropriate to apply these descriptions, and a huge periphery of relatively superficial engagement.
>
> (in R. Berger and McDougall 2011: 14).

So we can see from this 'heated debate' that there is agreement among media educators that the Internet is a big deal for changing media, but disagreement (or at least a degree of scepticism) over the ability of 'Web 2.0' to open up the media to greater access for all and the extent to which Media Studies should depart from its traditional ways of analysing media.

The ideas covered thus far have been from media academics, disagreeing over the implications of all this change for Media Studies. It's important, now, to consider some broader ideas that connect the subject to culture, politics, citizenship and economics:

WE MEDIA

In 2004, Gillmor presented the idea that 'Big Media' – News Corporation, CNN, the BBC, Google – have, up to now, exercised control over who gets to produce and share media, and the effect of this on democracy is that there is a 'concentrated' choice of media leading to profits for an 'oligopoly' (small cluster) of companies. But Gillmor saw the Internet as a catalyst for a challenge to this establishment hegemony as ordinary citizens use blogs and other online communication tools to share their own news, which he called 'citizen journalism'.

For Gillmor, bloggers are 'the former audience' and news blogs are a new form of people's journalism. He refers to blogs from Iraq that offered an alternative to the Western media's accounts; a range of collaborative wikispaces, children's news blogs and Persian networkers using the Internet for a collective voice in a country where free speech is curtailed:

> The spreading of an item of news, or of something much larger, will occur – much more so than today – without any help from mass media as we know it. The people who'll understand this best are probably just being born. In the meantime, even the beginnings of this 'shift' are forcing all of us to adjust our assumptions and behaviour.
>
> (Gillmor 2004: 42–3)

CASE STUDY: THE LONG TAIL

In 2006, Chris Anderson, editor of *Wire* magazine, published his theory – a description of the way that the Internet has transformed economics, commerce and consumption. His metaphor illustrated what had been happening for a few years since broadband was 'rolled out' to consumers. Whereas in the pre-broadband era, companies and distributors were interested in 'blockbuster' hits and best-selling products, now there is a realization that adding up all of the 'niche' consumption might amount to as much revenue as the units sold of the peak material. In other words, if you think about it in spatial terms, on a graph, there is a longer, flatter, low end of the market – a 'long tail'.

Anderson's idea was radical in persuading economists that, as broadband Internet allows more people to look for and share or buy a wider variety of material and products, what happens is that people buy less of more. So instead of ignoring all the small sales of obscure products in favour of concentrating on huge mass sales (more of less), businesses ought to consider both routes and give equal weighting to both ends of the tail:

> The theory of the Long Tail can be boiled down to this: Our culture and economy are increasingly shifting away from a focus on a relatively small number of hits (mainstream products and markets) at the head of the demand curve, and moving toward a huge number of niches in the tail. In an era without the constraints of physical shelf space and other bottlenecks of distribution, narrowly targeted goods and services can be as economically attractive as mainstream fare.
>
> (Anderson 2006: 52)

WIKINOMICS

Tapscott and Williams (2006) provide another 'big idea' about business and commerce in the online age. The subtitle of their intervention is 'How mass collaboration changes everything'. Understood in this way, Web 2.0 brings Media Studies and economics together:

> As people individually and collectively program the Web, they're increasingly in command. They not only have an abundance of choices, they can increasingly rely on themselves. This is the new consumer power. It's not just the ability to swap suppliers at the click of a mouse, or the prerogative to customise their purchased goods (that was last century). It's the power to become their own supplier – in effect to become an economy unto themselves.
>
> (Tapscott and Williams 2006: 46)

'Wikinomics' presents a set of key trends, that the authors observe taking place in the 21st century around digital online media. 'Peering' is the free sharing of material on the Internet, which is seen as good for business when it cuts distribution costs to almost zero but bad for people who want to protect their creative materials and ideas as 'intellectual property'. So the 'roar of collaborative culture' will change economics beyond recognition and corporations are forced to respond or perish. 'Free creativity' is a natural and positive outcome of the free market, so attempting to regulate and control online 'remix' creativity is like trying to hold back the tide. The happy medium is achieved by a service such as Creative Commons, which provides licences that protects intellectual rights whilst at the same time allowing people to remix content. 'Democratization' of media occurs when peering, free creativity and 'we media' journalism become the norm. 'Global thinking' is brought about by Web 2.0 in the sense that the Internet is the 'world's biggest coffeehouse', a virtual space in which a new blog is created every second. In this instantly global communication sphere, national and cultural boundaries are inevitably reduced. The accumulation of these observations is that the combination of three things – technology (Web 2.0), demographics (young people are described as 'digital natives' – they have grown up in a collaborative virtual world which to them is 'natural' and instinctive) and economics (the development of a global economy where business can, and must, think of its market as international, given that traditional, national production structures have declined as we have entered the 'knowledge economy') result in a 'perfect storm' that creates such a force that resistance is impossible, so any media company trying to operate without wikinomics as a mindset will be akin to a tiny fishing boat on the sea during this rare weather event.

This is a 'brave new world' thesis that attracts many critics and sceptics who respond with a counter-observation that the world is not changing as quickly and profoundly as Tapscott and Williams would have us believe. They think the idea of 'digital natives' assumes too much and that the 'wikinomics' argument ignores inequality and the fact that the vast majority of the world's population don't even have access to the affordances they blindly celebrate.

WETHINK

Charles Leadbeater's intervention develops this further – beyond business and consumption – to argue that the way we think and make sense of 'knowledge' is fundamentally shifting in the online age. For Leadbeater, open access knowledge-building communities on the web allow ideas to be shared and tested much more quickly and effectively. Ultimately this leads to us becoming more creative and innovative as we are liberated from the usual institutional constraints on how things get invented and changed by scientists and academics. Leadbeater uses *World of Warcraft* to make his point and extend it to challenge the world of education:

> In such games it's the players who create the content. A computer game with a million players only needs 1 per cent of them to create content for other players to use and the game has an unpaid development team of 10,000. If we could persuade 1 per cent of Britain's pupils to be player-developers for education, that would be 70,000 new sources of learning. But that would require us to see learning as something more like a computer game, something that is done peer to peer, without a traditional teacher.
>
> (Leadbeater 2008: 26)

FANDOM AND PARATEXTS

Fan media of various kind is a longstanding aspect of media reception that Media Studies hasn't paid sufficient attention to. The work of Matt Hills (2005, 2010) is essential in this area, and its relevance for this chapter lies in Hills' analyses of online *Dr Who* fan engagement. Whilst many of Hills' examples have nothing to do with 'Web 2.0' – Trekkies and Elvis impersonators, for example – it is clear that broadband Internet can accelerate fan interpretations and reimaginings of media products as is demonstrated by the vast array of 'mash up' and 'sweded' video content on YouTube. The result is that media producers now have to accept that fans can and will upload their own versions of material within hours of an official broadcast and in some cases, like *Dr Who*, the writers have explicitly built fan interaction into the dynamics of production, creating a 'hyperdiegetic' range of textual practices around the drama:

> Though a text like Doctor Who may seem to have obvious 'frontiers' in space and time, such as the bounded minutes of its broadcast, or its sell-through existence as a DVD, in Foucault's terms the text of Who is inevitably caught up in a system of references to other ... texts ... it is a node within a network ... It indicates itself, constructs itself, only on the basis of a complex field of discourse. It is thus as a node within a network of discourses that I will think about Doctor Who.
>
> (Hills 2010: 15)

Hills doesn't subscribe to any kind of 'Fandom 2.0' (my words) idea, but we can observe from his work that there is simply more fan activity to witness now that the internet creates a digital archive of the kind of interpretative and creative reception that was happening already but in less visible offline spaces. Jenkins (2006) has also paid serious attention to the ways that fans operate as 'textual poachers' and more recently Jonathon Gray (here in a blog conversation with Jenkins) has described the ways that, for online fan communities, the material surrounding the text is 'picked and mixed' in the assemblage of a unique version of the textual experience, thus adding to the notion that digital 'textual poaching' and fandom offer us visible 'reimaginings' of texts – he calls this *'paratextual'* activity:

> I wanted to focus on how one can use paratexts to cut one's groove through a text in a way that isn't necessarily working against the pro- ducer's version, but that is personalised nonetheless. Many relationship and character study fanvids, for example, don't necessarily repurpose a character, but they do ask us to stop and think about that character and his or her history in ways that the official text, in its breathless progression, may not have time to do. I don't mean to suggest that this is either the dominant form of fan use of paratexts, or even one that's necessarily changed in a more obviously convergent media era. But it might help cultural studies to back away from some of the desires for an Orcs v Hobbits style bad-and-good battle between The Industry and The Fans, and to focus on smaller, humbler moments of repurposing.
>
> (Gray 2010)

So, again, Gray helps us resist binary thinking (1.0/2.0 or 'the media'/'the audience') and encourages us to pay attention to the 'in between spaces' where the two sides of the coin are converging. Jenkins here makes the same observation:

> You say 'User Generated Content'. We say 'Fan Culture'. Let's call the whole thing off. The media industry and its consumers alike now operate as if moving towards a more participatory culture, but they have not yet agreed upon the terms of our participation. Even companies that adopt a collaborationist logic have a lot to learn about creating and maintaining a meaningful and reciprocal relationship with their consumers.
>
> (Jenkins 2006: 177)

CASE STUDY: LIFE WITHOUT MEDIA?

At a conference in Barcelona in 2011, media academics were asked to imagine such a world, without the role of media professionals as '**gatekeepers**' (see Chapter 3 on Powerful Media). This was a hypothetical endeavour, not a declaration that it has happened, but nevertheless this idea resonates with the other 'big ideas' dealt with in this chapter.

Taking two examples from the conference, we can observe two different poles of the 'media is changing' discourse – the implications for media change *for* 'the media' (opportunities and threats) and broader concerns about what media *does* to society.

Raphael (2011) discusses the potential of Web 2.0 to dispense with the idea of the mass media, finding that, in reality, big media have managed to harness social media to continue their hegemonic practices, but with new methods. Looking at the way that the 'share' option on websites and social networks allows for cross-advertising, Raphael cites the way that *Inception* (2010) was marketed virally by Leonardo DiCaprio's use of social media with the result that the film was the longest 'trending topic' on Twitter. This is hardly the 'end of big media'.

Toby Miller (2011) also muses on this through his discussion of 'empowered fans and empowered firms' in the new media era and sets up two competing discourses in this regard – a 'Marxist/ Godardian utopia' in which the culture industries are dismantled, set against the kind of 'lost world' rhetoric which he finds in William Gibson's novel *Pattern Recognition*:

> For us, of course, things can change so abruptly, so violently, so profoundly, that futures like our grandparents' have insufficient 'now' to stand on. We have no future because our present is too volatile. We have only risk management. The spinning of the given moment's scenarios. Pattern recognition.
>
> (Gibson 2003: 57)

For Miller, these competing discourses, taken together, view the future of media as 'simultaneously perfect and horrific'. His striking departure from both projections is to urge the field of Media Studies to consider the environmental implications of toxic digital waste – a materialist concern almost entirely ignored in the subject to date (in the linear and digital periods). His argument is that all of the claims for a more participatory, connected online society ignore the material environmental harm that could outweigh political or civic good in the abstract. Put another way, the metaphorical notion of 'the cloud' – where all of our digital information will be stored, freeing us up from carrying any tangible media of any kind – denies the material conditions, the 'digital footprint', which is as significant for the future of the planet as the 'carbon footprint' created by air travel. For Miller, Media Studies, in the wake of changing media, needs to develop a 'more materialist and ecological history of the present'.

AFTER THE MEDIA?

This idea – from Bennett et al. (2011) doesn't argue that the media has 'ceased to be' but, rather, that Media Studies might be well advised to carry on without it. In other words, the part of Gauntlett's 'Media Studies 2.0' that the authors concur with is the idea that Media Studies has been too focused on 'big media' and not sufficiently concerned with how people attribute meaning to media, re-interpret (and in some cases remix) media and 'map' media exchanges and meanings into their everyday lives.

This kind of Media Studies would look very different to the kind of textual analysis and audience research models that the subject has traditionally made use of. Studying media in this way would be process rather than content orientated. That is to say the focus of study would not be 'the text' but the tracing and analysis of textual fields, the choices individuals make as they negotiate 'myriad texts' and the 'common patterns' in their selections. The Media Studies teacher or lecturer, in this model, would be there to facilitate students in a critical reading of their own practices as textual agents – the 'mediated' nature of their own lives, but not 'the media' – defined as separate from, but determining aspects of their lives:

New media and technology do not provide in themselves a paradigm shift that necessitates new kinds of teaching. Instead we suggest that in fragmenting the idea of 'the media' as a construct, an object of study or an employment sector, these new digital media have simply opened our eyes to the already and always dubious nature of that idea.

(Bennett et al. 2011: 1)

Figure 5.1 3D TV – Resisting Binaries – Retro New Media?

NO BINARIES

Hepworth (2011), in an article about the renaissance in vinyl record collecting, observes the hybrid, convergent nature of his – and fellow collectors' – preferences for how they consume music in the digital era. People, he says, either want their music fast and portable or slow and cherished but often people find a place for both. Likewise, we sometimes want moving images on our mobile devices – tiny and portable – or on ★★★★-off (my words) massive screens with booming surround sound. Hepworth's main anecdote for his 'slow and quick, portable and tangible' duality is his enthusiasm for playing vinyl records and then tweeting the covers to readers of his magazine. Strangely perhaps, the 'neither one thing nor the other' status of the CD makes it seem likely to be a forgotten format in years to come, with music on the cloud for quick access and preserved on vinyl for its cherished antique status.

And so we keep returning to this challenge – resist binary thinking. Critical media students need to rise to this challenge and bear witness to the complexity of debates around the changing role of media in life. The extent to which 'Web 2.0' and social media affordances have made 'the media' (or our relationship with media) more democratic is one such area where the answer can't just be one or the other. Likewise, creating a binary opposition between the 'old media' (for example, newspapers) and 'new media' (such as citizen journalism in the shape of blogs) won't stand either. So when Cortina (2011), speaking at a conference where media academics responded to the question of 'life without media', asked 'can we have an enlightened society with new media?', she was setting up the new frontier of citizen media as 'other' to existing public sphere journalism and also dividing 'good rhetoric' (discussion, debate in context) from 'bad rhetoric' (communication that intends to manipulate and influence), evoking enlightenment philosophy to celebrate the existence of the 'good' and warn against the digital proliferation of the 'bad' in spaces where the mass media are not able to safeguard enlightened citizenship. We must bear in mind, however, and in particular with regard to the 'watershed moment' for the Rupert Murdoch empire in the UK in 2011, that the 'old media' are often attacked for their undermining of enlightened civic deliberation, as Alistair Campbell reminds us:

> It is a sad irony that we have more media coverage than ever, but less understanding or real debate.
>
> (Campbell 2007: xv)

Campbell is describing 'new media' here in terms of 24-hour news TV but he isn't referring to citizen journalism or 'we media' (Gillmor 2004). So when weighing up the contribution that new social media might be making to citizenship and democracy, we must avoid a rose-tinted view of the status quo just as clearly as we should refute the more conjectural claims of the 'Media 2.0' thesis.

HAPPY MEDIA?

We can go further with these critical questions about changing media. As well as asking whether or not (or, rather, the extent to which) we're more included, more interactive, more participative and more informed citizens in the online age, we might ask whether being more and more connected can actually make us happier. Returning to Alistair Campbell, as well as condemning the contemporary political media with which he did battle for years as Tony Blair's 'spin doctor', he has more recently developed a theory of happiness which, broken down, distinguishes between happiness 'on reflection' (which essentially can only be known at the end of your life) and happiness as experienced in the present tense. This latter feeling, he argues, is not acquired through achievement or fulfilment, as this is always deferred – we are, in effect, happiness addicts so when we experience pleasure, we seek more of it. It is certainly not achieved through wealth (very rich people tend to look back with nostalgia at the happier times during the struggle to become affluent or to seek even more wealth, but rarely are they content 'in the moment'). Happiness, he suggests, is experienced most often through being connected – to other people, causes, struggles (Campbell 2011).

HOW IS THIS RELEVANT TO THE STUDY OF CHANGING MEDIA?

Returning to Gauntlett (2011a), in *Making is Connecting*, Campbell suggests that new digital media have enabled people to be more creative and cites this as a gateway to increased happiness. He doesn't suggest that we weren't creative before, but that Web 2.0 has enabled us to be more quickly and collaboratively creative, and goes further to argue that the act of creativity is often in itself bound up with a desire to be connected, and that, whereas in the linear age this would take more effort and be more risky, digital social media now makes it possible for us to be creative and share our work with lower stakes and with some 'safety in numbers'. Both Gauntlett and Campbell reference the work of Richard Layard (2006), who produced a strategy for measuring happiness. This has also influenced the current UK Prime Minister David Cameron, who has introduced the measuring of happiness as a criteria for developing social policy. For Campbell, this is much needed as 'it's very hard to see how we can be happy as a nation when every day two million people buy the *Daily Mail*' (Campbell 2011). Layard's view is also that a sense of shared purpose is an essential criteria for happiness and is far more important than material wealth, achievement or status. Gauntlett describes creativity as a 'social glue', and uses Layard's criteria to consider the role of new media in promoting happiness:

> Happiness is strongly associated with the quality of our relationships and our connections with others. Happiness is heavily associated with self-esteem, and having projects to work on. Happiness has to be

worked towards, and it flows from action, not passivity. All of this suggests that creative projects, especially when either online, or offline but linked via online platforms, are invaluable for human happiness.

(Gauntlett 2011a: 223)

Defining creativity is no mean feat, of course. Ishiguro's *Never Let me Go* (2005) (recently adapted for cinema) is oft-cited by academics as a starting point, including Howard Gardner (the author of the theory of 'multiple intelligences') who, at a conference in Vancouver (2007) suggested that Ishiguro's narrative might be a starting point for a discussion about creativity as a form of intelligence. In the novel (and film), human clones being farmed for organ donation believe they can extend their existence beyond the set date for donation provided they have shown sufficient aptitude in such practices as art and music – these practices are assumed to be indicative of humanity: 'We took away your art because we thought it would reveal your souls. Or to put it more finely, we did it to prove you had souls at all.'

In many science fiction narratives where the human/machine distinction is blurred for dramatic effect, such acts of 'creative' expression are used in the plot to tease out questions of what it is to be human. The assumption is that creativity is something innately human, which perhaps cannot be replicated by a simulation of human 'spirit'. For a more conventionally academic 'take' on such ideas, see the report by Banaji and Burn (2006) on 'the rhetorics of creativity, the contributions made by Trotman (2007) and Readman (2011) on the dilemmas for educators seeking to 'pin down' creativity and McDougall and Trotman's analysis of 'digital creativity' (2011).

Notwithstanding the contested nature of creativity as an idea in academic discourse, Gauntlett's compelling idea that making things, being creative, intervening in culture in active ways, will promote happiness, is a lovely way to set up our final chapter – on 'making media'.

SUMMARY

This chapter has introduced you to a range of arguments and counter-arguments about the degree to which changes to media production and exchange in the context of online and social media developments require a 'paradigm shift' for Media Studies. There is no 'right answer' and the examples discussed will soon be replaced by new developments, so the critical media student must avoid binary assumptions about old and new, good and bad, empowering and controlling and find their own informed, academic path through these contested ideas.

The ideas and examples covered in this chapter can lead to the following summative statements:

★ The ideas of Marshal McLuhan about 'the medium is the message' and how our tools come to shape us now appear to be more relevant than at the time that he shared them.
★ Web 2.0 has led some media academics to develop a strategy for a 'Media Studies 2.0'.
★ The 'Media Studies 2.0' idea has been criticized by other academics for 'technological determinism'.
★ The idea that there is such a thing as 'the media' anymore has been challenged in this new media environment, with some academics questioning whether it/they ever existed in the first place.

FURTHER READING

All of the work referred to in this chapter is listed in the bibliography at the end of the book, but the key recommended reading on the material covered in this chapter is as follows:

Anderson, C. (2006) *The Long Tail*. London: Random House.
Contested but influential theory of the rise of niche media consumption in the online age.

Berger, R. and McDougall, J. (2011) 'Apologies for cross-posting: A keynote exchange', *Media Education Research Journal* 2(1), www.merj.info/MERJ% 202.1-Editorial.pdf.
Interview exchange between Henry Jenkins and other prominent figures on participation culture.

Gauntlett, D. (2011b) *Media Studies 2.0 and Other Battles Around the Future of Media Research*. Kindlebook.
Updated overview of the original theory, the subsequent debates and the author's response to critics of the idea.

Leadbeater, C. (2008) *We-think: Mass Innovation, Not Mass Production: The Power of Mass Creativity.* London: Profile, www.wethinkthebook.net/home.aspx
Another contested, but optimistic theory about how being connected online is changing the way we work.

McLuhan, M. (1994) *Understanding Media; The Extensions of Man.* London: MIT Press.
Always influential, but now heralded as prophetic.

6

MAKING MEDIA

AIMS

This chapter will introduce you to:

* The key 'verbs' of media practice taught in Media Studies;
* Approaches to critical, reflexive practical learning;
* Documentary making as an example of 'ethnographic' work that links theory to practice.

MEDIA PRACTICE

As we have seen, it's relatively easy to make media and find an audience these days. Practical work in Media Studies differs from 'everyday' media creativity in its focus on professional standards and critically reflexive processes that put media theory into practice. The main areas of professional-standard reflexive practice that Media Studies 'trains' are as follows:

WRITING

Writing for journalism (in legal, ethical and critical frameworks), writing for the screen, writing for the web, writing for radio, writing for game design. Conventions of storytelling, narrative and modes of address.

WORKING WITH STILL IMAGES

Researching, designing, mocking up, composing, framing, lighting, capturing, editing, sharing and theorising the meaning in/of still images in professional, legal and ethical contexts.

WEB DESIGN

Writing in HTML, site design, navigation protocols, multimodal design, facilitating interaction, aesthetics and features of working with still and moving images.

WORKING WITH MOVING IMAGES

Researching, planning, storyboarding/scripting, composing, framing, lighting, shooting, editing, sharing and theorizing the meaning of moving images in narrative sequence in professional, legal and ethical contexts.

ANIMATION

All of the above (animation 'bridges' still and moving image work) with the addition of drawing, physical modelling or 3D computer-generated imaging.

GAME DESIGN

Writing for games, managing rule economy, 2D and/or 3D design, coding, enabling 'modding' where appropriate/desired and features of working with still images, moving images, animation and web design as required.

AUDIO PRODUCTION

Researching, planning, scripting, capturing (recording – live or pre-recorded), editing, mixing, post-production for recorded sound, sharing and theorising the meaning of audio.

The above 'inventory' is, in practice, contextualized in most cases by collaborative activity, so a media student will specialize in particular aspects of each 'skillset', which mirrors the media industries in which, usually, professionals work on similar roles (for example, camera, modelling for games, writing for the web) across productions.

If you've read the book in a linear fashion you will know that there is a lot of scepticism about the notion that media students in the second decade of the 21st century are 'digital natives' who instinctively know how to use non-linear media production technology. In order to resist falling into this trap, it's wise to conduct a 'digital skills audit' before starting practical work.

SKILLS AUDIT

To do this, simply identify the key technical/creative skills you will need to successfully complete a production outcome. For a short film these might be things such as camerawork and video editing, soundtrack composition and graphic design, screen performance and directing. Alongside these 'hard' skills, you will need to consider personal, learning and thinking skills such as creative thinking, groupwork and self-discipline.

Whatever set of required skills you focus on, you should think of an example of a piece of creative work you have undertaken outside of education that relates to those given techniques. For each example, you rate how highly you would assess your expertise as demonstrated by the process or outcomes (or both).

You can, from this, produce an 'audit', which consists of a statement about each of the required creative skills explaining what you can bring to this new project in terms of previous experience. This can be illustrated by examples from your 'everyday creativity' or images and weblinks that signpost skills.

This can form the agenda for the first production meeting for the project in hand. You can refer to these audits, with your co-creatives, for assigning roles, making the case for a particular role based on demonstrable skills gained from past experiences – this is good preparation for managing your 'employability'. As you develop as a student of media, you can update your audit, not only because of the necessity to employ different skills and techniques for different tasks, but also to add new examples from previously completed coursework or recent projects you've been engaged with outside of your course.

THE VERBS OF MEDIA PRACTICE

Going back to Prensky's (2010) helpful separation of nouns from verbs, and his focus on the latter for contemporary media education, the rest of this chapter will introduce the key verbs that are used to make meaning, regardless of how the nouns might change. So the chapter will not provide soon to be out of date information about particular kinds of software or equipment. Instead it will run through some key areas in which theory and practice combine in creative meaning-making in Media Studies.

IMAGINING

Media Studies might seem 'high tech' but the creative skill of meaning-making is not. To illustrate this, Nick Potamitis (in McDougall and Potamitis 2010) uses building toys from the 1960s with his media students to get them into collaborative and creative 'making' – here we combine those skills in one term, 'imagining' how things might be made. Students – who have only just been introduced to one another for the first time – are invited to work in small groups to build a model house from Bayko, a children's construction toy from the 1960s. There are a number of fan-sites that feature Bayko kits, such as www.melright.com/bayko/. The students are faced with three problems in attempting to complete the task. Firstly, Bayko is an unfamiliar system to them, it consists of thin metal rods that must be slotted into plastic bases to support individual bricks and doors and window frames to create the walls of the buildings and so is unlike either Lego or Meccano building systems with which they may have more experience. Second, students have insufficient initial information to complete the task, as they are given no written instructions or diagrams to help them build their model, their only reference point being an illustrated image on the cover of the box. Third, the students have limited component parts with which to work, each group beginning the task with only some of the requisite pieces needed to complete the building and a surplus of other pieces that they may not need to use. So, in order to complete the task, each group will have to work together to make sense of Bayko, learn quickly how the pieces interlock, try out alternative designs and ideas, start over when things go wrong, organize their resources and their roles within the group, and negotiate with other teams to swap pieces, tips and ideas. As such they need to put personal, learning and thinking skills into action, and the activity provides a 'low-stakes' opportunity for students to constructively overcome frustrations and challenges in many ways very similar to those they will face in their 'real' Media Studies coursework.

PLANNING

One key distinction between 'prosumer' media exchange and the professional practice taught in Media Studies is the focus on research and planning. Starting from research into existing, professionally produced and distributed media products, audience awareness and planning deadlines, the generation of simple ideas informed by this research is more sensible than great ambition. A combination of simplicity and originality is the key to a successful project, alongside rigorous attention to detail. In the case of video, planning the minute details of each shoot meticulously to avoid wasting time on location, testing batteries, lighting and microphones before setting off and planning to improvise when group members are absent are all essential criteria. These points might seem mundane but they are very important. Rigorous attention to detail, planning, health and safety and time management, despite appearances, allow creativity to flourish:

> Treat your project with professionalism and organisation and you will not go far wrong! Enjoy your work. Being creative is brilliant – but you can't beat being organised.
>
> (Fraser 2002: 42)

TELLING

Before doing anything with a videocamera, lighting kit, microphone and tripod, try making a three-shot film with a packet of jelly babies, a pack of Post-It notes and any other items you have in your possession. Assuming you will use the sweets as people, the challenge is to construct a meaningful narrative that tells a story through a combination of framing, point of view and 'anchoring' captions on the Post-Its. Test out the three-shot film with a friend and see how much of the story they can work out from your outcomes. You will find that it is much easier to tell a story in this way than you might think and this activity reinforces the fact that three quarters of the meaning of a media text is constructed by the audience – who imagine they can 'join the dots' of the meaning that they infer from the information provided. This also reinforces (back to the verbs) the fact that storytelling skills are more important than technical abilities – the latter can be picked up very quickly but the former are developed out of life experience and observation.

Storytelling can be the missing 'glue' in Media Studies coursework, without which student projects come unstuck because they simply aren't very interesting. Consider these three ideas about storytelling from the 'Story' conference, convened by journalist Matt Locke in 2011 at which writers, journalists and creative media professionals gathered to discuss storytelling as an 'art'. Firstly, Phil Gyford is spending his time representing the Pepys diaries as tweets, to see if the storytelling craft can be remediated in this way (www.pepysdiary. com/). Secondly, Karl James (who manages The Dialogue Project) said that the most important element in telling a story is listening to other people in order to learn about how people understand the world. Asking questions, and resisting the temptation to fill the silence, is crucial. Kathryn Corrick took pictures of people's shoes as a kind of 'semiotic way in' to their stories. These are just three contrasting examples of approaches to telling stories from a much more diverse annual conference – see http://thestory.org.uk/ for more, but the point is that critical and creative media students need to take the idea of storytelling very seriously before they think about the technical tools for so doing.

There is a high premium, in this era of cheap and easy to use technology, on producing work that attracts an audience. But we have seen that good storytelling is certainly as important, and probably more so, than technical or aesthetic qualities in 'getting attention' (these days information is abundant, attention is scarce (Lilley 2009). Alongside the everyday affordances of YouTube, grassroots, community and campaign media co-exists, produced by volunteers – a more old fashioned form of 'prosumer'. One such group of video activists, which will be of more or less interest depending on your political persuasion, is Reel News (www.youtube.com/user/ReelNews), providing 'news from the front line', making commissioned campaign videos for activists or training them to make films for themselves.

IMAGING

Sometimes this verb is replaced by 'capturing' but imaging extends this phase to include pre-production conceptions about what to film/shoot/record. A useful activity to prepare for imaging is 'storyboarding in reverse'. The starting point of any production work regardless of the medium – print, film, radio or the web – should always be the trusty pencil and paper. Whether it is sketching thumbnails for a storyboard, drawing key-frames for an animatic, outlining a rough website design or plotting the intersections of different narrative strands in a radio-play, it is important to get used to 'thinking with your hands' early on without being overly concerned about being 'able' to draw. The 'reverse storyboard' involves watching a sequence of a film and then producing a rough sketch of each shot by hand before jotting down some key observations. Drawing each image forces you to look more closely and to attend to the spatial composition and relationships within the frame and between the different shots in a way that doesn't happen just by watching without engaging the hand. Depending on the length of the sequence you may want to focus on some key shots rather than all of them.

This exercise is excellent preparation for your own storyboarding, as you will have observed the detail of different camera-angles and framings. Next, you can use the Art of the Title website (www. artofthetitle.com) as a template and, then, rather than trying and storyboard an entire sequence consecutively, sketch out what you consider to be nine key frames for a title sequence, music video or trailer. These nine starting points can later expand into a full storyboard with further shots to fill the gaps.

DESIGNING

Once again, technology is a tool with which to realize more fundamental principles of design. Media students need to develop 'design thinking' and the only resource required to start out is (again) a pack of Post-It notes. Working collaboratively on an 'idea shower' for a response to a media project brief, each member of the production team initially jots down as many thoughts and ideas as possible onto notes, however wide of the mark those ideas might seem at first, operating in as free and fluid a way as you can. The ideas need not be expansive – just keywords or quick sketches. These are then displayed and explained. During the meeting the notes are moved, clustered, removed, re-arranged, new ones added so that particularly interesting or innovative ideas get developed and expanded upon and connections start to be formed between a whole raft of possible ideas. The wall can be subsequently maintained as an ongoing resource and you can refer back to it to see how you learn from alternative ideas, recombining previous suggestions into more creative and successful combinations.

EDITING

Regardless of what software you use to realize your editing, the most important principle at work is nothing to do with technology – it's literacy, how will a sequence make meaning for/by an audience through a combination of information and inference? Editing is about making critical and intelligent choices – what to include, what to delete, how to crop, how to sequence and how to 'anchor' (with soundtrack or music) and how to connect through transitions which are either unobtrusive (the 'invisible glue' of meaning) or symbolic (dialectical montage). One fundamental, if ironic, principle is this – the more sophisticated the editing software, the better it will be at making the editing LESS noticeable.

THEORIZING

The difference between everyday media work (for example, videos posted on YouTube), professional media work and Media Studies is praxis – the combination of theory and practice. Production work in Media Studies isn't about a linear putting of one into the other, it's to do with putting them together so you can't tell where one ends and the other begins. Will your media product reinforce or challenge conventions, the dominant ideology, storytelling principles, modernist ideas about representation? Will it be ethnographic (the outcome of spending time in the lived experience of those it repre-sents) or will it construct an 'other' through its subject/object dynamics? Will it simply appeal to a 'target audience' or will it work within a more fluid arrangement of paratextual diegesis. Are you a producer, a fan, or both? What are the ethical implications of your contribution to media culture?

LEARNING

Media Studies should not just be about taking a critical distance from 'the media' so we can be less vulnerable to its influence. Nor should it just be a vocational 'training route' into the media industries, without any critical consideration of the implications of how the news is constructed according to an agenda or how videogames represent women. Media Studies, like any academic subject, is about learning. As the subject is increasingly framed by 'transmedia' practice, storytelling that cannot be reduced to media specific silos, it's strategically helpful to summarise Henry Jenkins' key principles for transmedia education (2010) in relation to production processes in Media Studies.

How is the media you produce a product of spreadability and drillability? The first idea is about dispersal − scanning across the media landscape to find meaning. The second is about looking more deeply (drilling down) into a particular subject in detail. Learning should combine the two, and your praxis − production work that is theoretically charged − should demonstrate range and detail in this way. How does your media work relate to continuity (of 'classic' conventions and highly influential existing media texts) and multiplicity (the need for cultural plurality, different interpretations, alternative readings, remix)? Next, does your work create immersion (in a virtual domain, perhaps), does it build a world and allow for new ways of imagining culture, or is it fixed in a stable existing view of reality? How have you applied principles of seriality − the dispersal of stories in sections or units which are compelling in themselves but also challenge and engage the 'reader' to return? How have you dealt with subjectivity − looking at the same thing from different points of view? Have you embraced this as a healthy part of plurality, or attempted to lay down an objective truth? Finally, your work is performance. What are you being asked to do with what you are being taught? How are you adapting this from knowledge to skill? How is this adaptation an act of improvisation − akin to how fans demonstrate their understanding through different kinds of performances. How has your media work created a space where you are able to perform the Media Studies curriculum in ways which are meaningful to your life − as a cultural activator?

Figure 6.1 Cultural Activators

CASE STUDY: A METHODOLOGY FOR ETHNOGRAPHIC DOCUMENTARY

THE TASK

* Produce a documentary video that represents perceptions of local, national, and global identity in your local area.
* Participants in the documentary will articulate their feelings about their identities as citizens in a changing, arguably more 'global' culture and share their ideas about what their local area will be like in the year 2112.
* You must plan and realize the documentary in a way that gives participants the maximum opportunity to articulate these feelings and perceptions without leading them to a particular view.
* Your planning must take full consideration of ethical issues and the process must be ethnographic so that the participants speak for themselves.

Reflexive media literacy is achieved through combining technical skills (digital competence), communication skills, initiative (meticulous research and planning, attention to detail and designing), entrepreneurship (consideration of audience and how to engage people), social and civic competences (understanding of political, economic, ethical and legal frameworks) and cultural awareness and expression (telling stories and making meaning).

The production of an ethnographic social documentary allows for these competences to be realised and for media literacy to be enhanced through praxis, using Jenkins's (2010) principles of transmedia education as a framework.

Digital **ethnography** (see Wesch 2011) adopts the well-established ethnographic methodology – immersion in specific locations and cultures in order for research to be situated within contexts as opposed to observed from outside, with the use of new media to allow students of media to act as media producers and researchers at the same time in virtual ways and across geographical boundaries.

The task is to produce a video documentary on any aspect of local or national identity in the ethnographic mode (without the conventional use of voice-over or other framing devices that speak on behalf of participants). In so doing, social documentary is a reflective tool – as opposed to merely a 'media product' that necessarily adopts existing institutional conventions – so that participants in the documentary can directly reflect and comment upon their perceptions of their identities as more or less individual, local, national, and global. This will include articulation of how they imagine their local area to change in the next 100 years. This digital ethnography will capture the 'lived experience' of citizenship.

PLAN

Who will take each role on the production? How will the producers work with the subjects (peers) to ensure an ethnographic approach? Who will be the subjects? Which existing documentaries inform the approach, and how will the documentary, in its ethnographic form, challenge conventions of 'objective' documentary? What are the access routes to the participants, how will consent be secured, how will the material be 'triangulated' – shown to the participants prior to dissemination? What will be the locations? How will open-ended questions be posed? What is the desired cultural and demographic range (in ethical contexts and with an understanding of representation)? How will appropriate sound and lighting be achieved in the locations? What are the contingency plans for unforeseen problems? What are the planned timings for stages of the data collection?

CAPTURE

Low-tech filming (flip cameras) of a sufficient range of raw footage from which to edit to the required documentary length and meet the objectives of the ethnographic project. Footage must be appropriately lit and audio must be clear. Framing and composition must suit the intended *mise en scène*.

EDIT

Critical storytelling principles inform choices made about inclusion and exclusion, sequencing, narrative construction, combination of elements in demographic and cultural contexts, 'anchoring' voice-over and music. Editing should be an 'invisible glue' where unobtrusive continuity is required and demonstrate literacy skills where symbolic 'dialectical montage' is intended to convey meaning.

SHARE

Following appropriate 'triangulation' and consent, the film should be disseminated online to invite playback and comment/paratextual exchange and reworking where appropriate.

REVIEW

The documentary will be critically evaluated as: a) an exploration of documentary conventions; and b) a piece of ethnographic research on the theme of identity in global contexts.

LEARN

Using the transmedia education framework and key competences for critical media literacy, students should reflect on how the process and outcomes have enabled learning about their own identities in relation to ideas about place, culture, citizenship and storytelling. Key elements will be immersion, multiplicity, drillability, subjectivity and performance.

PRAXIS

This approach is an example of praxis in its combining of a range of theoretical perspectives (documentary conventions, theories of identity, theoretical principles of storytelling, continuity and narrative) with key learning competences (skills) and an ethnographic method which enables richer consideration of 'voice' and representation. Theory and practice are thus inter-related at every stage of the methodology.

SUMMARY

This chapter has introduced you to the kinds of technical, creative and reflective skills that Media Studies teaches. It has connected theory and practice at all times and focused on the 'verbs' (skills) which stay constant rather than the 'nouns' (software, hardware, technologies) as these outdate quickly. That said, a 'transmedia' approach does combine theory and practice in a way which recognises contemporary media exchange as being more convergent and fluid. The ideas and examples covered in this chapter can lead to the following summative statements:

* Creative media production work is a process of praxis – combining theory and practice.
* Careful research and planning and attention to detail are essential elements of creative media production.
* High quality media production is the outcome of high quality storytelling.
* Critical students of media need to reflect on the ways in which media production processes enable deep 'drilling down' into questions of plurality, subjectivity and identity – these deeper issues separate Media Studies practical work from professional training and 'everyday' media exchanges.

GLOSSARY

AESTHETIC In media education, usually understood as one type of code amongst several, the aesthetic domain describes *visual* language in cultural contexts.

AFFORDANCES Describes opportunities (usually new ones) provided by new forms of technology or online spaces.

ANCHORAGE The 'pinning down' of meaning through image being placed in relation to text, or vice versa. The shipping metaphor suggests a wild sea of potential meaning, with the sign (boat) needing to be motivated through grounding.

AUDIENCE An umbrella term for the person or people reading any media text. Digital technology has led to increasing uncertainty over how we define an audience, with general agreement that the notion of a large group of people, brought together by time, responding to a text, is outdated. Furthermore, advocates of 'Media 2.0' claim that the way people engage with culture is now the 'concept formally known as the audience'. See the journal *Participations* for contemporary research in this domain.

AVATAR An on-screen icon or representation of the user/player in a computer game or virtual world. Now in the everyday lexicon as a result of the James Cameron film.

BINARY Western thought, it is said, is framed by a tendency for us to think in opposites – for example, old/new, rather than embrace ambiguity and difference. In digital coding, binary describes the coding of digits as noughts and ones.

BRICOLAGE The construction of meaning through remixing a combination of elements to make a new style. Ranges from sur-realist work where things are deliberately put out of context to postmodern media where there is no sense of 'original' material to worry about as everything new is made up of a bricolage of the old – what was already there.

CITIZENSHIP The role of a person in a contemporary democracy is described in this way and the critical student of media assesses role of the media in constructing us as modern citizens and in enabling enlightened citizenship (see Cortina 2011).

CONVENTIONS The repeated, normative practices expected within a culture. In the context of Media Studies, we are con-cerned with the normative elements of a particular type of media text that come to be expected within genres.

CONVERGENCE Hardware and software coming together across media, and companies coming together across similar boundaries, to make the distinction between different types of media and different media industries increasingly dubious. Also, the way that media access is now multi-modal – for example, watching TV on an iPhone, and the means that social media affords us new opportunities to be creative and/or participative – is described by Henry Jenkins as 'Convergence Culture'.

CRITICAL Asking questions, not taking things for granted, seeking to analyse the reasons for seemingly 'common sense' ideas about people and the world.

CULTIVATION The notion that over time, media images grow ideas in our minds about groups of people. We don't directly think of ourselves as influenced by these but there may be a subconscious effect on, for example, ideas regarding women's body image or young black males wearing 'hoodies'.

CULTURAL CAPITAL From Bourdieu and Passeron (1990). Symbolic acquisition that can be exchanged, including qualifications, knowledge, family background, taste, values and other non-material forms of status.

CULTURAL IMPERIALISM Within broader discussions of globalization, the practice of dominant groups and nations imposing their cultural preferences and claims to legitimate knowledge on other people and nations. Hollywood is the classic example.

DECONSTRUCTION At its simplest, taking apart texts at the 'micro' level to see how they work to make 'macro' meaning. At the more complex level, students investigate intertextuality and ways in which texts can only be understood in relation to other texts.

DEMOCRACY Society founded on equality, in which the decision-making powers are elected and are thus representative and accountable. Whether the media is democratic is a very different question, as we do not elect newspaper owners such as Rupert Murdoch or powerful producers such as Simon Cowell, for example.

DEMOGRAPHIC Breaking down society or a sample of people by characteristics such as age, gender, ethnicity, occupation, income and socio-economic status (quantitative means).

DIALECTICAL An exchange of points of view, or propositions (theses) and counter-propositions (antitheses) resulting in the creation of new ideas, which are then new propositions to be countered (a such dialectical thinking is infinite).

DIASPORA The process by which people who are dispersed around the world take elements of their culture with them so that the cultural imperialism model is disrupted by people using media in relation to hybrid identities. See Ruddock (2007).

DIEGESIS Describes what is present in the world of a text, as opposed to the extra bits (such as soundtrack or voice-over) that exist only for the audience.

DIGITAL NATIVES From Prensky (2010), the idea that young people, being born into a digital world, are 'at home' there, local to it, whereas the older generation are 'migrants'.

DISCOURSE A coherent system of speaking, thinking and understanding, in language. Systematically organized ways of using language to order the world, from Foucault (1988).

ELLIPSIS What is left out of a narrative, but remains in the story.

EMANCIPATION Freedom from oppression. In Media Studies, new technologies – if they seem to offer an enhancement to democracy and access to the public sphere, can be hailed as 'emancipatory'. In some ways, Media Studies itself is seen this way – challenging the media hegemony through critical media literacy.

ETHICS Issues of morality (always up for grabs). Often different to legal considerations, an important distinction.

ETHNOGRAPHY A research method that involves spending time in the specific situation the research participants operate in, so the 'data' is grounded in their real experience rather than being observed from the outside.

FALSE CONSCIOUSNESS Marxist term describing a state of being in which individuals are happily distracted from the truth (by ideology) and are thus convinced, or at least prepared to accept, that things are as they have to be.

FEMINISM Often misunderstood as an 'extreme', militant politics, feminism is nothing more outrageous than the belief that we should oppose media texts that represent women as inequal to men, or as mere unthinking objects for male scrutiny. There are a wide range of types of feminism with more political, symbolic or textual approaches.

FLOW A state of mind that happens when we are involved in activity that is at once challenging and pleasurable and incrementally more difficult. Associated with videogames especially.

FOUCAULTIAN An approach influenced by the work of Michel Foucault – seeking to analyse discourse and how language 'delimits' ways of thinking about ourselves and the world around us, to understand 'the technology of the self'.

FRANKFURT SCHOOL Marxist school of thought, featuring Adorno, concerned mainly with ideology and the role of mass media (the culture industry) in reinforcing hegemony and manufacturing consensus.

FRIVOLITY Playful behaviour, where things are not taken seriously and thus challenged and subverted.

GATEKEEPING The role played by editors, producers, owners and regulators in opening and closing, to greater and lesser extents, the flow of media information through processes of selection and construction.

GENRE A French term for 'type', widely used in subjects that analyse texts to describe categories of texts and their shared properties (conventions).

GLOBALIZATION The idea that a proliferation of digital technology, deregulation and convergence combine to allow multinational and cross-cultural media production and consumption within a global economic system founded on the free market. A contested idea.

GLOCAL Global media adapted to suit a local context. The global and the local working together.

GRAND NARRATIVES These are belief systems that provide their followers with a whole overarching sense of the meaning of life or a manifesto for change. Religions, philosophies and political movements can be understood as grand narratives or, in other words, 'big stories'.

HEGEMONY A process by which people in power create the impression that their view of the world is neutral and the most 'common sense' view to take.

HYBRID A fusion of more than one media form or a mixing of global and local or a mixing of identities.

HYPERREALITY A state in which images, and simulations, take on more reality than the state they represent, so that the distinction between reality and representation is no longer sustainable. From Baudrillard (1998). See also **virtual** and **postmodern**.

IDENTITY Culture and discourse construct subjects (from Foucault 1988), so for Media Studies the task is not so much to consider the relationship between texts and identities taken on by individuals as to analyse the plurality of identities that subjects play with and the ways in which these are mediated and increasingly virtual.

IDEOLOGY A dominant set of ideas presenting itself as common sense or truth. Power relations are reinforced through ideology. Marx, Althusser, Gramsci and Chomsky are key writers in this area.

IMMERSION Used in analysis of videogames, in two ways. Firstly, perceptual (the senses are dominated by the experience of the game) and secondly, psychological (the player is drawn into the game in the imagination).

INTERACTIVE Media texts which offer audiences the opportunity to shape the text in some way. Not necessarily the same as democratic (see Turner 2010).

INTERPELLATION The misrecognition of oneself in a media text (from Althusser 1977) – for example, women or men recognizing, in magazines or advertising, an idea of their gender which was not their construction.

INTERTEXTUAL The chain of signification, in which texts always make overt or more subtle references to one another. All language is intertextual, and as all experience in culture is languaged, hence reality becomes intertextual by nature.

LIFEWORLD The network of experiences of families, hobbies, social gatherings, leading to culturally transmitted ways of understanding the world.

LONG TAIL Chris Anderson's idea (2006) that the large amount of niche markets are now worth as much as the smaller amount of big markets.

LUDOLOGY The study of play.

MALE GAZE From Laura Mulvey (1975), an analysis of media images that suggests that the camera represents a male perspective, and as such casts men as subjects and women as objects.

MARGINALIZATION A process by which groups of people are excluded from mainstream discussion or representation. Not direct prejudice but a more subtle form of marking people out as 'different' or 'other'.

MACRO Big broad themes, issues and debates. Critical media students need to relate 'micro' examples to these big, broad 'macro' themes.

MARXIST All theory derived from the works of Marx, founded on a belief that the ruling classes in any time and place maintain their economic and systematic power through controlling not only the means of production but also culture and ideology. Marxist theory, traditionally, seeks to expose the falsity of dominant ideology and reveal the truth previously obscured, and as such it has empowerment of the alienated as its primary objective.

MEDIA ACCESS Describes the degree of ease with which citizens can be seen and/or heard in the media and respond to the media and be provided with a dialogue with institutions, and the amount of opportunities evident for people to produce media texts themselves and for them to be distributed – clearly this is greatly increased by social media but not necessarily by reality TV – see Turner (2010).

MEDIA LANGUAGE An umbrella term to describe the ways in which audiences read media texts through understanding formal and conventional structures (for example, the grammar of film editing). So media literacy describes our ability to read and write in this extended sense of language.

MEDIASPHERE John Hartley used this term to describes a 360-degree environment for media consumption, which fundamentally changes how we need to think about media audiences.

MEDIA STUDIES 2.0 A response to Web 2.0, proposed by Will Merrin (2006) and then by David Gauntlett (2007), in which the role of online user generated content and sharing is seen as fundamental to how we understand media audiences. This makes it mandatory for Media Studies to change how it operates. The subject of a 'heated debate' and by no means a generally accepted idea among media teachers and academics.

MEDIATION The idea that our everyday lives are so woven together with media that our existence is 'mediated' – we cannot separate 'the media' from 'life'.

MEME An idea, or creative item, that is passed on virally from person to person to the point where lots of people know about it and are talking about it.

METALANGUAGE When we are able to step outside of language to analyse meaning rather than just using language to make meaning, we have a metalanguage. This is an advanced form of literacy.

MICRO A small, specific example.

MICROPOLITICS The way that small, seemingly insignificant decisions and interactions amount to outcomes that impact on people's lives.

MISE EN SCÈNE Everything that is put into the frame (essentially considering the paused moving image as a still image). Includes set design, location, costume, actors and make-up, non-verbal communication, colour and contrast, lighting and filter. Primarily an aesthetic practice.

MMORPG Massively Multiplayer Online Role Playing Games. For example, *World of Warcraft* and *Club Penguin*.

MODE OF ADDRESS How a text, in any media, speaks to its audience.

MORAL PANIC Exaggerated media response to the behaviour of a social group. A phrase coined by Stanley Cohen in 1972, this refers to overstated reactions to seemingly deviant aspects of popular culture, usually mobilised by the mass media. More recently, videogames have been the subject of widespread moral panics and they are often blamed for declining moral standards in general as well as specific cases of violent behaviour and tragedy. Social networking is also the subject of a moral panic.

MULTILAYERED Meaning that can be interpreted on many different levels. All media is multi-layered, when we drill down to the detail, but the term commonly describes texts which have been explicitly constructed with different readings or more and less complex interpretations as an intention.

MULTIMODAL A form of semiotics, multimodal theory attempts to understand the way that human communication mixes together a variety of forms and how it simultaneously represents, orientates and organizes by establishing relations between people. Has in recent years influenced the field of 'new literacies'.

MYTH From Roland Barthes, who analysed the way that dominant ideas in a culture take on the status of myth, so they appear natural and neutral. In semiotics, signs and symbols when added together amount to a system of myths.

NARRATOLOGY The study of videogames as stories – usually seen as in conflict with ludology, which foregrounds the study of games as play.

NEWS AGENDA The observation that a particular news provider will select and construct news within a framework influenced by political, corporate, cultural and commercial objectives. Brought very much to public attention in the UK in 2011 by the *News of the World* phone-hacking scandal.

THE 'OTHER' Through marginalisation, exclusion or representation, a group of people are marked out as exotic, alien or different to 'the norm'.

PARADIGM A framework of understanding scientific or cultural phenomenon. All messages, of any kind, are selected from paradigms. A 'paradigm shift' describes the point at which the usual ways of comprehending culture become outdated.

PARODY A text which does not simply imitate the style of another (pastiche) but instead is transformative in that it either mocks or shifts in some way the original text's conventions.

PLAYBACK 'Prosumer' media being viewed online, sometimes with comments as a 'feedback loop' among peers.

PLURALITY The degree to which there is space for a broad range of perspectives to be heard and a broad range of groups have access to media and can represent themselves in media. In a democracy, plurality of media ownership and access should be evident.

POLYSEMY This describes a plural range of possible meanings that audiences can interpret from texts. The more abstract and open-ended, the more polysemic the text is said to be. However, all media texts are open to interpretation and active reading so we might argue that all media meaning is polysemic.

POPULAR CULTURE Culture which is consumed by a wide range of people, as opposed to a smaller group, configured in some way as an elite, tends to be described as popular and this implies a derogatory view of tastes.

POSTMODERN Postmodernists believe that it is no longer sensible to describe media texts in terms of how they represent real life or events, but instead we should see reality as increasingly mediated, so the boundaries between reality and media-reality are blurred. The most famous postmodern philosophers are Jean-François Lyotard who described 'the postmodern condition' and Jean Baudrillard who wrote about this blurring of reality and simulation, which he called 'hyperreality'.

PROLIFERATION A significant and sustained increase in something.

PROPAGANDA The deliberate use of information to persuade large groups of people of the legitimacy of political or military action. Associated with totalitarian governments who use media and other information providers to manipulate public opinion.

PROSUMER The consumer becomes the producer.

PROTECTIONIST An approach to media which sees it as having harmful effects, against which people should be protected either through regulation or education. Media literacy is sometimes presented as a protectionist strategy.

PUBLIC SERVICE Founded on principles of democracy as opposed to profit. Avoid overstating binary oppositions between public service and commercial media, however.

REALISM A variety of ideas about the degree to which, and the variety of ways in which, media texts represent an idea of reality. There are a range of 'realisms': social realism, classical narrative realism, neo-realism, magical realism.

RECEPTION Contemporary audience theory is concerned with audience response and reaction and subsequently our understanding of a text's meanings emerge more from attention to audience interpretation than producer intent.

REGULATION The surveillance and the threat of action by organizations – sometimes governmental, sometimes from industry – leading to a degree of self-regulation on the part of media institutions and actual punitive measures in response to self-regulation breaking down. Regulation is sometimes economic, sometimes cultural and always political. There are always calls for more or less media regulation.

REPRESENTATION Media do not offer a transparent 'window' to reality but offer instead a mediated representation of it. The processes by which audience members come to understand media texts in terms of how they seem to relate to people, ideas, events, themes and places.

SEMIOTICS The science of signs and symbols from linguistics and structuralism. The analysis of 'units of meaning' (signs) in terms of their connotations within cultural myth systems.

SIMULATION The artificial imitation of an experience or a process with the intention of making the imitation as close as possible to the 'real thing'. Baudrillard and Zizek are key thinkers. See **virtual**.

SOCIO-CULTURAL Describes considerations of how our social experiences and cultural choices combine and how meanings are constructed by audiences through experience as much as through any fixed, intended, preferred messages from producers' points of view.

SPECTATORSHIP How a reader of moving images behaves, which will be culturally specific. So watching a film is not a practice that can be described as though it is a universal experience.

STRUCTURALISM An academic approach to analysing meaning as structured like language. Semiotics and narrative theory are two areas of Media Studies that are informed largely by structuralism.

SYMBIOSIS Two forms arranged in an interactive, organic relationship. Used to describe relationships between different media products.

TECHNOLOGICAL DETERMINISM When technology is seen as in itself the reason for a development.

TEXT Texts carry meaning that is constructed and Media Studies looks at texts in order to deconstruct them. All media products are texts. But we can extend this term to include people, ourselves and others – anything that is made up of a range of signs that are decoded and interpreted by people.

TRANSGRESSIVE A practice which transcends conventional approaches, and either subverts these existing ways of working, or challenges their value.

TRANSMEDIA See Jenkins (2010) – an approach to studying and making media that recognizes convergence and sees media production as being 'spread out' across different types of media forms.

VERISIMILITUDE The logical, seemingly authentic world of a text. Not the same as 'realist', because every text has a logical, sensible world constructed through continuity, detail and recognition. *Harry Potter* has verisimilitude but is not claiming to mirror our social reality.

VIRTUAL A simulation of the real. Whether we can any longer distinguish the real from the virtual and whether experience is the new reality, is an important question in contemporary Media Studies.

WEB 2.0 The term is from Tim O'Reilly and it describes the second phase of the Internet where the focus shifts from people receiving information and services to people creating and sharing material. Defined by collaboration, social networking and the democratic development and distribution of content by ordinary people.

WE MEDIA An adaptation of Gillmor's *We, the Media* (2004). Describes members of the public creating media that challenge the mainstream media hegemony. For Gillmor, the best example is 'citizen journalism'.

WIKINOMICS Tapscott and Williams (2006) coined this term to describe the impact of Web 2.0 on economics as well as media.

BIBLIOGRAPHY

Acosta, D. (2008) 'The "Telenovela" as a springboard for public debate', www.ipsnews.net/Africa/nota.asp?idnews=42978.

Adorno, T. (1991) *The Culture Industry*. London: Routledge.

Adorno, T. W. and Horkheimer, M. (1973) *Dialectic of Enlightenment*. Stanford: Stanford University Press.

Al-Jenaibi, B. (2007) 'Al-Jazeera and media pressure', *Global Media Journal* 6(10).

Allatson, P. (2004) 'The virtualization of Elián González' in *M/C Journal* 7(5), http://journal.media-culture.org.au/0411/16-allatson.

Althusser, L. (1977) *Lenin and Philosophy and Other Essays*. London: New Left Books.

Altman, R. (1999) *Film/Genre*. London: BFI.

Anderson, C. (2006) *The Long Tail*. London: Random House.

Appignanesi, R. and Garratt, C. (2004) *Introducing Postmodernism*. Cambridge: Icon.

Bacon, J., Mader, R. and Klick, K. (2010) 'Lady Gaga as postmodern feminist?', www.authorstream.com/Presentation/Kklick1564-375048-lady-gaga-post-modern-feminist-postmodern-feminism-entertainment-ppt-powerpoint, accessed 9 December 2011.

Banaji, S. and Burn, A. (2006) *The Rhetorics of Creativity: A Review of the Literature*. London: Creative Partnerships.

Barker, M. and Petley, J. (eds) (1998) *Ill Effects: The Media/Violence Debate*. London: Routledge.

Barlow, D. and Mills, B. (2009) *Reading Media Theory*. Harlow: Pearson.

Barlow, J. (1996) *A Declaration of the Independence of Cyberspace*, https://projects.eff.org/~barlow/Declaration-Final.html.

Barrett, P. (2006) 'White thumbs, black bodies: Race, violence and neoliberal fantasies in Grand Theft Auto: San Andreas', *The Review of Education, Pedagogy and Cultural Studies* 28: 95–119.

Barthes, R. (1984) *Mythologies*. London: HarperCollins.

Baudrillard, J. (1998) 'The Precession of the Simulacra', in J. Storey (ed.) *Cultural Theory and Popular Culture: A Reader* 2nd Edition: 350–57.

Bauman, Z. (1998) *Globalisation: The Human Consequences*. London: Polity.

Bazalgette, C. (2009) 'Literacy in time and space', in *Points of View* 1. London: Media Education Association.

Bazalgette, P. (2005) *Billion Dollar Game: How Three Men Risked it All and Changed the Face of Television*. London: Time Warner.

Benn, T. (2010) *Letters to my Grandchildren: Thoughts on the Future*. London: Arrow.

Bennett, P., Kendall, A. and McDougall, J. (2011) *After the Media: Culture and Identity in the 21st Century*. London: Routledge.

Berger, J. (1990) *Ways of Seeing*. London: Penguin.

Berger, R. and McDougall, J. (2010) 'Media education research in the twenty first century: Touching the void', *Media Education Research Journal* 1(1).

——(2011) 'Apologies for cross-posting: A keynote exchange', *Media Education Research Journal* 2(1).

Berners-Lee, T. (1999) *Weaving the Web: The Past, Present and Future of the World Wide Web*. Orion, London.

Bolas, T. (2009) *Screen Education: From Film Appreciation to Media Studies*. Bristol: Intellect.

Bourdieu, P. (1984) *Distinction: A Social Critique of the Judgement of Taste*. London: Routledge.

Bourdieu, P. and Passeron, J. (1990) *Reproduction in Education, Society and Culture*. London: Sage.

Brabazon, T. (2007) *The University of Google*. Aldershot: Ashgate Publishing

Bragg, B. (2006) *The Progressive Patriot: A Search for Belonging*. London: Bantham Press.

Branston, G. and Stafford, R. (2010) *The Media Student's Book* 5th edition. London: Routledge.

Brooks, L. (2010) 'Exotic, extreme, engrossing – tune in to channel poverty', *Guardian* 28 May.

Buckingham, D. (2003) *Media Education: Literacy, Learning and Contemporary Culture*. London: Polity.

——(2007) *Beyond Technology: Children's Learning in the Age of Digital Culture*. London: Polity.

——(ed.) (2008) *Youth, Identity and Digital Media*. Cambridge, MA: MIT Press.

——(2010a) 'Do we really need Media Education 2.0: Teaching media in the age of participatory culture', *Journal of Media Literacy* 57(1–2): 18–27.

——(2010b) 'The future of media literacy in the digital age: Some challenges for policy and practice', *Media Education Journal* 47: 3–10.

——(2011) *The Material Child: Growing up in Consumer Culture*. London: Polity.

Buckingham, D. and Willet, R. (eds) (2010) *Video Cultures: Media Technology and Everyday Creativity*. London: Palgrave Macmillan.

Buckingham, D. et al. (2008) *Literature Review for the Bryon Report*. London: Government.

Burn, A. and Parker, D. (2003) *Analysing Media Texts*. London: Continuum.

Butler, J. (1990) *Gender Trouble: Feminisms and the Subversion of Identity*. Routledge: London

Byron, T. (2008) *Safer Children in a Digital World*. London: DCMS.

Campbell, A. (2007) *The Blair Years*. London: Hutchson.

——(2011) 'Happiness', the Thomas Baggs Lecture, University of Birmingham, 12 July.

Castro, F. (2010) *Reflections of Fidel*, - http://monthlyreview.org/castro.

Chomsky, N. (2002) *Media Control: The Spectacular Achievements of Propaganda*. New York: Seven Stories.

Chun, W. (2006) *Control, Freedom, Power and Paranoia in the Age of Fiber Optics*. Cambridge, MA: MIT Press.

Cohen, S. (1972) *Folk Devils and Moral Panics*. Oxford: Martin Robertson.

Cortina, A. (2011) 'Vida sin illustracion', keynote speech at Life Without Media, Barcelona: Universitat Remon Llull.

Csikszentmihalyi, M. (1996) *Creativity, Flow and the Psychology of Discovery and Intervention*. New York: Harper Perennial.

Cunnane, S. (2011) 'Direction of travel raises hopes of US–Cuban détente', *Times Higher Education* 14 July.

Curtis, A. (2011) *All Watched Over by Machines of Loving Grace*. BBC2 Documentary, May.

Davies, N. (2009) *Flat Earth News*. London: Vintage.

De Certeau, M. (1988) *The Practice of Everyday Life*. Berkeley: University of California Press.

de la Fuente, E. (2011) 'Signs and wonders', *Times Higher Education* 2 June.

de Zengotita, T. (2005) *Mediated: How the Media Shape Your World*. London: Bloomsbury.

Dixon, S. (2011) *Politics 2.0*. Stirchley: British Oak Press.

Dovey, J. and Kennedy, H. (2006) *Game Cultures: Computer Games as New Media*. Maidenhead: Open University Press.

Dyer, R. (1980) *Stars*. London: British Film Institute.

Dyja, E. (2010) *Studying British Cinema: The 1990s*. Leighton Buzzard: Auteur.

Easthope, A. and McGowan, K. (2004) *A Critical and Cultural Theory Reader*. Milton Keynes: Open University Press.

Elster, J. (1986) *Karl Marx: A Reader*. Cambridge: Cambridge University Press.

Fairclough, N. (1995) *Media Discourse*. London: Edward Arnold.

Fenton, N. (2011) 'We need more than a public enquiry', *Red Pepper* 8 July.

Fikiciak, M. (2004) 'Hyperidentities: Postmodern identity patterns in massive multiplayer online role playing games' in J. Wolf and B. Perron (eds) *The Videogame Theory Reader*. London: Routledge.

Fiske, J. (1987) *Television Culture*. London: Methuen.

Forrest, A. (2011) 'Blurred vision', *Big Issue (Scotland)*, 23-29 May: 22–3.

Foucault, M. (1980) *Power/Knowledge: Selected Interviews and Other Writings 1972–1977* (edited by C. Gordon). London: Harvester.

——(1988) *Technologies of the Self: A Seminar with Michel Foucault* (edited by L. H. Martin, H. Gutman and P. H. Hutton). Amherst: University of Massachusetts Press.

Fraser, P. (2002) 'Production work tips', *Media Magazine* 1. London: English and Media Centre.

——(2011) 'Web 2.0 and media education', *Life Without Media Conference Proceedings*. Barcelona: Universitat Ramon Llull.

Fraser, P. and Wardle, J. (2011) *A Manifesto for Media Education*, www.manifesto formediaeducation.co.uk.

Fuller, M. (2007) *Media Ecologies: Materialist Energies in Art and Technoculture*. Cambridge, MA: MIT Press.

Gardner, H. (2007) 'Creativity and intelligence', keynote presentation to Imaginative Education Conference. Vancouver: Simon Fraser University.

Gauntlett, D. (1998) 'Ten things wrong with the "effects model"' in R. Dickinson, R. Harindranath and O. Linne (eds) *Approaches to Audiences*. London: Edward Arnold.

——(2002) *Media, Gender and Identity – An Introduction*. London: Routledge.

——(2007) *Creative Explorations: New Approaches to Identities and Audiences*. London: Routledge.

——(2009) 'Media Studies 2.0: A response', *Interactions: Studies in Communication and Culture* 1(1): 147–57.

——(2011a) *Making is Connecting*. London: Polity.

——(2011b) *Media Studies 2.0 and Other Battles Around the Future of Media Research*. Kindlebook.

Gauntlett, D., McDougall, J., Readman, M. and Trotman, D. (2011) 'Making is connecting: Extended review', *Media Education Research Journal* 2(1).

Gee, J. (2000) 'Discourse and sociocultural studies in reading' in M. L. Kamil, P. B. Mosenthal, P. D. Pearson and R. Barr (eds) *Handbook of Reading Research Volume III*. Mahwah, NJ: Lawrence Erlbaum Associates.

——(2003) *What Videogames Have to Teach us about Learning and Literacy*. Basingstoke: Palgrave Macmillan.

Gibson, W. (2003) *Pattern Recognition*. London: Penguin.

Gillmor, D. (2004) *We, The Media*. California: O'Reilly.

Gilroy, P. (2004) *After Empire: Melancholia or Convivial Culture?* London: Routledge.

Goffman, E. (1990) *The Presentation of Self in Everyday Life*. London: Penguin.

Goldkorn, J. (2006) *Al Jazeera: Global Change in the Media Environment*, www.danwei.org/tv/global_change_in_the_media_env.php, 25 November.

Goldsmith, B. (2010) *Local Hollywood: Global Film Production and the Gold Coast*. St Lucia: University of Queensland Press.

Gott, R. (2009) 'It's time to let Cuba in from the cold', www.guardian.co.uk/commentisfree/2009/jan/02/barack-obama-cuba-fidel-castro.

Gray, J. (2010) *On Anti-Fans and Paratexts*, interview with Henry Jenkins, http://henryjenkins.org.

Habermas, J. (1974) 'The public sphere: An encyclopedia article', *New German Critique* 3(1): 49–55.

Hafez, K. (ed.) (2008) *Arab Media: Power and Weakness*. London: Continuum.

Hall, S. (1980) 'Encoding/Decoding' in S. Hall, D. Hobson, A. Lowe and P. Willis (eds) *Culture, Media, Language*. London: Hutchison.

——(2009) 'The rediscovery of ideology', in J. Storey (ed) *Cultural Theory and Popular Culture: A Reader* 4th edition. London: Pearson: 111–41.

Hall, S. and du Gay, P. (eds) (1996) *Questions of Cultural Identity*. London: Sage.

Hartley, J. (2007) *Television Truths*. London: Blackwell

Hawkes, T. (1977) *Structuralism and Semiotics*. London: Routledge.

Helsby, W. (2005) *Understanding Representation*. London: Routledge.

——(2010) *Studying Reality TV*. Leighton Buzzard: Auteur.

Hepworth, D. (2011) 'Shelf life', *The Word* 101.

Hermes, J. (2009) 'Audience Studies 2.0: On the theory, politics and method of qualitative audience research', *Interactions; Studies in Communication and Culture* 1(1): 111–27.

Hills, M. (2002) *Fan Cultures*. London: Routledge.

——(2005) *How to Do Things with Cultural Theory*. London: Hodder.

——(2010) *Triumph of a Time Lord: Regenerating Doctor Who for the Twenty-First Century*. London: I. B. Taurus.

Hindman, M. (2006) *The Myth of Digital Democracy*. Princeton: Princeton University Press.

Hoggart, R. (1967) *The Uses of Literacy*. London: Chatto and Windus.

Horkheimer, M. and Adorno, T. (2001) 'The culture industry: The enlightenment of mass-deception', in M. Durham and D. Kellner (eds) *Media and Cultural Studies: Keyworks*. Oxford: Blackwell.

Humm, M. (ed.) (1992) *Feminisms: A Reader*. London: Harvester Wheatsheaf.

Illich, I. (1973) *Tools for Conviviality*. London: Calder & Boyars.

Irvine, S. (2006) 'Globalisation and media education', *In the Picture* 54.

Ishiguro, K. (2005) *Never Let Me Go*. London: Faber & Faber.

Jarvis, J. (2009) *What Would Google Do?* London: Collins.

Jarvis, P. (2010) *Learning to Be a Person in Society*. London: Routledge.

Jay, M. (1984) *Adorno*. London: Fontana.

Jencks, C. (2005) *Culture*. London: Routledge.

Jenkins, H. (2006) *Convergence Culture: Where Old and New Media Collide*. New York: New York University Press.

——(2010) *Transmedia Education: The 7 Principles Revisited*, http://henryjenkins.org.

Johnson, S. (2005) *Everything Bad is Good for You*. London: Penguin.

Kabir, N. (2001) *Bollywood: The Indian Cinema Story*. London: C4 Books.

Kallioniemi, K., Kärki, K., Mäkelä, J. and Salmi, H. (eds) (2007) *History of Stardom Reconsidered*. Turky: International Institute for Popular Culture.

Kardish, L. (2004) 'Cuba V: The challenge of the next generation', http://history.sundance.org/films/204.

Kendall, A. and McDougall, J. (2009) 'Just gaming: On being differently literate', *Eludamos: Journal for Computer Game Culture* 3(2): 245–60.

Khan, J. (2010) 'Why did I back Wikileaks?', *Guardian: After Wikilieaks* 5 February: 25.

Kress, G. (2010) *Multimodality: A Social Semiotic Approach to Contemporary Communication*. London: Routledge.

Kung, L., Picard, R. and Towse, R. (2008) *The Internet and Mass Media*. London: Sage.

Lacey, N. (2010) *Image and Representation* 2nd edition. London: Macmillan

——(2011) 'Culture or culchure: Who decides what's best?', *Media Magazine* 35.

Lambie, G. (2008) 'Reinventing the revolution', *International Journal of Cuban Studies* 1(1): 138–9.

Lanier, J. (2011) *You are Not a Gadget: A Manifesto*. London: Penguin

Lankshear, C. and Knobel, M. (2006) *New Literacies: Everyday Practices and Classroom Learning*. Maidenhead: Open University Press.

Laughey, D. (2007). *Key Themes in Media Theory*. Maidenhead: Open University Press.

Lawton, R. and Cortes, C. (2010) 'The new media ecology: Towards a taxonomy of the web-based media', *Journal of Media Literacy* 57(1–2): 15–17.

Layard, R. (2006) *Happiness: Lessons from a New Science*. London: Penguin.

Leadbeater, C. (2008) *We-think: Mass Innovation, Not Mass Production: The Power of Mass Creativity*. London: Profile.

Leggott, J. (2008) *Contemporary British Cinema: From Heritage to Horror*. London: Wallflower.

Lemish, D. (2006) *Children and Television: A Global Perspective*. London: Blackwell.

Lievrouw, L. (2011) *Alternative and Activist New Media*. Cambridge: Polity

Levinson, P. (2001) *Digital McLuhan: A Guide to the Information Millennium*. London: Routledge.

Lilley, A. (2009) 'The attention wars: Inaugural lecture', Centre for Excellence in Media Practice, Bournemouth University, www.cemp.ac.uk/activities/inaugurallecture.php, accessed 13 December 2011.

Lister, J. (ed.) (2009) *New Media: A Critical Introduction* 2nd edition. London: Routledge.

Livingstone, S. (2009) *Children and the Internet: Great Expectations, Challenging Realities*. London: Polity.

Lovink, G. and Riemens, P. (2010) 'Ten theses on Wikileaks', *Network Cultures*, http://networkcultures.org/wpmu/geert/2010/08/30/ten-theses-on-wikileaks.

Lull, J. (2006) *Media, Communication, Culture: A Global Approach*. Cambridge: Cambridge University Press.

Lyotard, J. (1984) *The Postmodern Condition*. Manchester: Manchester University Press.

MacPherson, C. (1966) *The Real World of Democracy*. Oxford: Oxford University Press.

Marsh, J. (ed.) (2005) *Popular Culture, Media and New Technologies in Early Childhood*. London: Routledge.

Mason, P. (2011) 'Murdoch: The network defeats the hierarchy', *Guardian* 10 July.

McDougall, J. (2010) 'Wiring the audience', *Participations*.

McDougall, J. and O'Brien, W. (2008) *Studying Videogames*. Leighton Buzzard: Auteur.

McDougall, J. and Potamitis, N. (2010) *The Media Teacher's Book* 2nd edition. London: Hodder.

McDougall, J. and Smythe, G. (2010) 'Barefoot interview', *Points of View* 3, http://themea.org/2010/barefoot-interview, accessed 9 December 2011.

McDougall, J. and Trotman, D. (2011) 'Real audience pedagogy: Creative learning and digital space', in J. Sefton-Green and K. Jones (eds) *The Routledge International Handbook of Creative Learning*. London: Routledge: 273–82.

McLuhan, M. (1994) *Understanding Media: The Extensions of Man*. London: MIT Press.

McMahon, B. et al. (2011) 'What News Corps owns', *Guardian* 16 July.

McMillin, D. (2007) *International Media Studies*. London: Blackwell.

Merrin, W. (2005) *Baudrillard and the Media*. Cambridge: Polity.

——(2006) 'Media Studies 2.0: Upgrading and open-sourcing the discipline', *Interactions: Studies in Communication and Culture* 1(1).

Mill, J. S. (1986) *Utilitarianism*. London: Fontana.

Miller, T. (2006) *A Companion to Cultural Studies*. London: Blackwell.

——(2011) 'Life without media', keynote speech at Life Without Media conference, Barcelona 30 June.

Moores, S. (2005) *Media/Theory*. London: Routledge.

Morley, D. (1981) '"The *Nationwide* audience": A critical postscript', *Screen Education* 39: 3–14.

Morozov, E. (2011a) *The Net Delusion*. London: Allen Lane.

——(2011b) 'The age of the Wikileaks-style vigilante geek is over', *Guardian* 5 February.

Mullen, L. (2009) 'Estate of mind', *Sight and Sound* October.

Mulvey, L. (1975) 'Visual pleasure and narrative cinema', *Screen* 16 March.

Murphy, P. and Kraidy, M. (eds) (2005) *Global Media Studies*. London: Routledge.

Murray, A. (2011) 'Caught with their trousers down', *Morning Star* 16 July.

Murray, R. (2008) 'The New Social Realism', *Splice: Studying Contemporary Cinema* 2(2).

Naughton, J. (2010) 'Thinking like an ecologist', keynote session at Media Education Summit, Birmingham, 7 September, www.cemp.ac.uk.

——(2011) 'Thanks Marshall, I think we've finally got the message', *Observer* 24 July.

Neale, S. (1999) *Genre and Hollywood*. London: Routledge.

Newman, J. (2004) *Videogames*. London: Routledge.

Oates, S. (2008) *An Introduction to Media and Politics*. London: Sage.

Open Net (n.d.) 'Internet in Cuba', http://opennet.net/sites/opennet.net/files/cuba.pdf.

Perullo, A. and Fenn, J. (2007) 'Language ideologies: Choices and practices in Eastern African hip hop', in H. Berger and P. Carroll (eds) *Global Pop, Local Language*. Mississippi: University Press of Mississippi.

Pilger, J. (2001) 'The Crusaders', *New Internationalist* 333.

Plato (1987) *The Republic*. London: Penguin.

Porter, H. (2011) 'Over more than three decades, no one dared question the perversion of politics by and for Rupert Murdoch', *Observer* 10 July.

Postman, N. (1998) *Five Things We Need to Know About Technological Change*, www.mat.upm.es/~jcm/neil-postman–five-things.html.

——(2006) *Amusing Ourselves to Death: Public Discourse in the Age of Showbusiness*. London: Penguin.

Prensky, M. (2010) *Teaching Digital Natives: Partnering for Real Learning*. Four Oaks: Corwin Press.

Press, A. and Williams, B. (2010) *The New Media Environment: An Introduction*. Oxford: Wiley-Blackwell.

Puttnam, D. (2011) 'We must seize this chance to ensure a free and diverse media', *Observer* 10 July.

Rabinov, P. (ed.) (1984) *The Foucault Reader*. London: Penguin.

Ramone, J. (2011) *Postcolonial Theories*. London: Palgrave Macmillan.

Raphael, J. (2011) 'Mass media reboot: "The Internet triumphs"' in *Life Without Media: Conference Proceedings*. Barcelona: Universitat Ramon Llull.

Readman, M. (2011) 'Inspecting creativity: Making the abstract visible', *Media Education Research Journal* (2:1): 57–72.

Rehak, B. (2003) 'Playing at being: Psychoanalysis and the avatar', in J. Wolf and B. Perron (eds) *The Videogame Theory Reader*. London: Routledge.

Rheingold, H. (2003) *Smart Mobs: The Next Social Revolution*. New Work: Basic Books.

Robertson, R. (1994) 'Globalization or glocalization?', *Journal of International Communication* 1(1): 33–52.

Robinson, P. (2002) *The CNN Effect*. London: Routledge.

Rosenberg, H. and Feldman, C. (2008) *No Time to Think: The Menace of Media Speed and the 24 Hour News Cycle*. London: Continuum.

Ruddock, A. (2007) *Investigating Audiences*. London: Sage.

Said, E. (1995) *Orientalism*. New York: Random House.

Sánchez, Y. (2011) *Generación Y*, http://desdecuba.com/generaciony, accessed 13 December 2011.

Sarder, Z. and Van Loon, B. (2000) *Introducing Media Studies*. New York: Totum Books.

Scannell, P. (2007) *Media and Communication*. London: Sage.

Schiller, D. (1997) *Digital Capitalism: Networking the Global Market System*. Cambridge, MA: MIT Press.

Shelton, R. (2003) *No Direction Home: The Life and Music of Bob Dylan*. US: Da Capo Press.

Shirky, C. (2009) *Here Comes Everybody: How Change Happens When People Come Together*. London: Penguin.

——(2011) 'The whistleblowing site has created a new media landscape', *Guardian: After Wikilieaks* 5 February: 2.

Siebert, F. S., Peterson, T. and Schramm, W. (1963) *Four Theories of the Press*. Chicago: University of Illinois Press.

Smith, P. J. (2001) 'Blood of a poet', *Sight and Sound*, June: 30–1.

Stafford, R. (2010) 'Do we have to live like this? The concept of change in Media Studies', *Media Magazine* 34.

Stald, G. (2008) 'Mobile identity: Youth, identity and mobile communication media', in D. Buckingham (ed.) *Youth, Identity and Digital Media*. Cambridge, MA: MIT Press.

Stern, S. (2008) 'Producing sites, exploring identities: Youth online ownership', in D. Buckingham (ed.) *Youth, Identity and Digital Media*. Cambridge, MA: MIT Press.

Storey, J. (ed.) (2009) *Cultural Theory and Popular Culture: A Reader* 4th Edition. New York: Longman.

Strinati, D. (1995) *An Introduction to Theories of Popular Culture*. London: Routledge.

Suwito, K. (2011) 'The (new) face of Indonesia: Revealing the postcolonial identity on Facebook' in *Life Without Media: Conference Proceedings*. Barcelona: Universitat Ramon Llull.

Tagg, J. (1988) *The Burden of Representation*. London: Palgrave Macmillan.

Tapscott, D. and Williams, A. (2006) *Wikinomics: How Mass Collaboration Changes Everything*. London: Atlantic Books.

Taylor, P. (2010) *Zizek and the Media*. London: Polity.

Thussu, D. K. (2007) *Media on the Move: Global Flow and Contra-flow*. London: Routledge.

Trotman, D. (2007) 'Liberating the wise educator: Cultivating professional judgment in educational practice', in A. Craft, H. Gardner and G. Claxton (eds) *Creativity, Wisdom, and Trusteeship: Exploring the Role of Education*. Thousand Oaks: Corwin Press: 158–66.

Turner, G. (2010) *Ordinary People and the Media: The Demotic Turn*. London: Sage.

Tyrell, H. (1988) 'Bollywood in Britain', *Sight and Sound* August.

Venegas, C. (2010) *Digital Dilemmas: The State, the Individual and Digital Media in Cuba*. London: Rutgers University Press.

Villarejo, A. (2007) *Film Studies: The Basics*. London: Routledge.

Waters, M. (1995) *Globalization*. London: Routledge.

Watson, J. and Hill, A. (2003) *A Dictionary of Communication and Media Studies*. London: Hodder Arnold.

Wesch, M. (2009) *The Machine is (Changing) Us: YouTube Culture and the Politics of Authenticity*, www.youtube.com/user/mwesch.

——(2011) *Digital Ethnography*, http://mediatedcultures.net/ksudigg, accessed 13 December 2011.

West, D. (1995) 'Strawberry and chocolate, ice cream and tolerance: Interview with Tomás Gutiérrez Alea', *Cineaste* 21(1–2): 16–19.

Whittam-Smith, A. (2011) 'Who's in control? Not just governments, that's for sure', *Independent* 26 May.

Wikipedia (2011) *Open Source Political Campaign*, http://en.wikipedia.org/wiki/Politics_2.0.

Williams, R. (2009) 'The analysis of culture', in J. Storey (ed.) *Cultural Theory and Popular Culture: A Reader* 4th edition. London: Pearson: 32–40.

Willis, P., Jones, S., Canaan, J. and Hurd, G. (1990) *Common Culture: Symbolic Work at Play in the Everyday Cultures of the Young*. Buckingham: Open University Press.

Winship, J. (1987) *Inside Women's Magazines*. London: Pandora.

Wintour, P. and Sabbagh, D. (2011) 'Privacy laws in chaos as MP names Giggs over injunction', *Guardian* 24 May.

Wolf, J. and Perron, B. (2003) *The Video Game Theory Reader*. London: Routledge.

Wright, E. (2002) *Senses of Cinema: Wong Kar Wai*, www.sensesofcinema.com/contents/directors/02/wong.html, accessed 9 December 2011.

Zizek, S. (1992) *Looking Awry: An Introduction to Jacques Lacan through Popular Culture*. Cambridge, MA: MIT Press.

——(2002) 'Welcome to the desert of the real', in A. Easthope and K. McGowan (eds) *A Critical and Cultural Theory Reader*. Maidenhead: Open University Press.

WEB RESOURCES

Clearly the Internet is an almost infinite resource, so trying to 'pin down' online resources for students of media is difficult and subject to being outdated. That said, here is a 'top 20' of useful current sites for Media Studies:

BRITISH FILM INSTITUTE – EDUCATION RESOURCES

www.bfi.org.uk/education
Provides a range of study materials for aspects of cinema and television related to Media Studies.

FILM EDUCATION

www.filmeducation.org
Provides a range of study materials for the academic study of films.

THE CASE FOR GLOBAL FILM

http://itpworld.wordpress.com
Very useful blog offering a theoretical perspective on world cinema.

THE CENTRE FOR EXCELLENCE IN MEDIA PRACTICE

www.cemp.ac.uk
Part of Bournemouth University, follow the links to interviews and presentations related to their annual Media Education Summit and the Media Education Manifesto.

DIGITAL STUDENT

www.guardian.co.uk/digitalstudent
A wealth of articles on technology and its uses in education.

DIGITAL YOUTH

http://digitalyouth.ischool.berkeley.edu/about
A project exploring how children are using digital media in their everyday lives.

DAVID GAUNTLETT

www.makingisconnecting.org
Gauntlett is a prolific user of the web to share his work so this is a portal to a vast array of interesting videos, articles and links to related academic work.

HENRY JENKINS

www.henryjenkins.org
Henry Jenkins' blog covers theories about fandom, participation and new media.

JOURNAL OF COMPUTER GAME CULTURE

www.eludamos.org/index.php/eludamos
Online academic articles on videogames.

JULIAN McDOUGALL ON TWITTER

twitter.com/JulianMcdougall
The author of this book tweets a regular stream of case study examples to test out media theories.

MEDIA EDUCATION ASSOCIATION

http://themea.org
Subject association for Media Studies.

MEDIA MAGAZINE

www.englishandmedia.co.uk/mm/index.html
Useful online material for A-Level and undergraduate Media students. *Media Magazine* also publishes student articles.

JOHN NAUGHTON – THE NETWORKER

www.guardian.co.uk/technology/series/networker
Useful blog from journalist covering technology and culture.

NETWORKS

www.adm.heacademy.ac.uk/resources/publications/networks-magazine
Online journal for the Higher Education subject centre for Media.

NEWSWIPE

www.youtube.com/watch?v=qpVTUdfcEMg
Charlie Brooker's satirical work has a lot to offer the critical student of contemporary media.

PARTICIPATIONS

www.participations.org
Journal publishing extensive and accessible online articles on the theories of audience, culture and change.

PETE'S MEDIA BLOG

http://petesmediablog.blogspot.com
Another portal to a vast range of useful material, from legendary media educator Pete Fraser.

TED TALKS

www.ted.com/talks/clay_shirky_how_cellphones_twitter_facebook_can_make_
    history.html
Essential resource. This example is Clay Shirky talking about social media.

UNTANGLING THE WEB

www.guardian.co.uk/technology/series/untangling-the-web-with-aleks-krotoski
Blog from Alex Krotoski, the journalist behind the BBC's *Virtual Revolution* series.

MICHAEL WESCH

www.youtube.com/watch?v=TPAO-lZ4_hU
This online lecture is one of many very interesting contributions. This link is a starting point to lots of others.

INDEX